Village i
SOMERSET

Anne-Marie Edwards

COUNTRYSIDE BOOKS
NEWBURY, BERKSHIRE

First published 1999
© Anne-Marie Edwards 1999

COUNTRYSIDE BOOKS
3 Catherine Road
Newbury, Berkshire

ISBN 1 85306 552 8

Designed by Graham Whiteman
Maps by Trevor Yorke
Photographs by Mike Edwards
The front cover picture is of Luccombe
and that on page 3 is of Winsford.

Produced through MRM Associates Ltd., Reading
Printed by J. W. Arrowsmith Ltd., Bristol

Village Walks
in
SOMERSET

Contents

AREA MAP SHOWING LOCATION OF THE WALKS

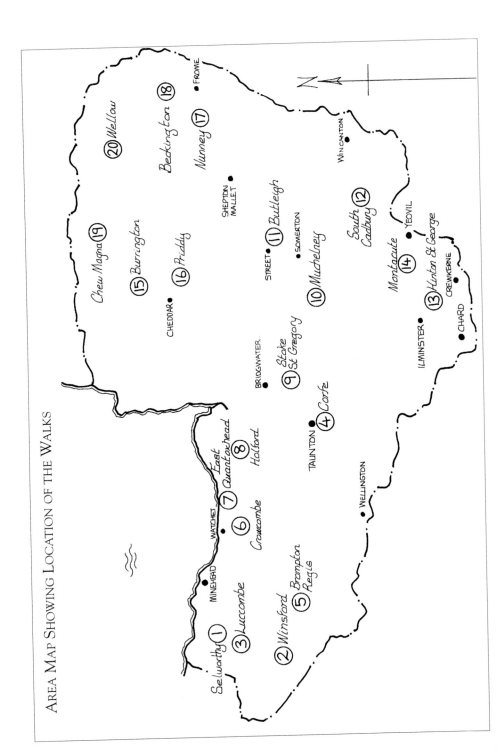

WALK

For our friends Captain Dickie Snell and his wife Liz.

Publisher's Note

We hope that you obtain considerable enjoyment from this book; great care has been taken in its preparation. Although at the time of publication all routes followed public rights of way or permitted paths, diversion orders can be made and permissions withdrawn.

We cannot of course be held responsible for such diversion orders and any inaccuracies in the text which result from these or any other changes to the routes nor any damage which might result from walkers trespassing on private property. We are anxious though that all details covering the walks are kept up to date and would therefore welcome information from readers which would be relevant to future editions.

Introduction

Somerset, the 'land of summer' tucked away in the West of England, is a paradise for walkers. Explore the countryside on foot and you will discover a quiet world characterised by amazingly varied scenery, unspoilt towns and villages and a rich store of history, legend and tradition.

There is no possibility of a dull walk in this fascinating county - Somerset offers everything a walker could wish for. The dramatic coastline rises to over 1,000 feet, the highest cliffs in England. Five ranges of hills, the Mendips, the Quantocks, the Poldens, the Blackdowns and the Brendons provide wonderful walking and spectacular views. A great plain known as The Levels, one of Europe's most important wetlands, forms the heart of the county. Far to the west the county can claim a very different landscape for most of Exmoor, still a wilderness of heather-covered uplands and deep leafy combes, lies within its bounds. Now Somerset has regained the Avon valley more recent attractions are found south of the river. Reservoirs created to supply Bath and Bristol have become delightful lakes with wooded shores threaded by footpaths. And the porous limestone of the Mendip Hills has resulted in spectacular caves and gorges where the earliest evidence of man has been found.

But glorious scenery is only part of Somerset's charm. The underlying rocks which give the county its natural beauty have supplied excellent building stone. In the south and east a whole village may be built of limestone quarried from Ham Hill, varying in colour from creamy white and grey, to yellow, gold, and brown ochre.

Throughout the county, mansions and churches are built of this glowing stone and in distant villages it is used to frame doors and windows. In the Mendips the most attractive villages are again built of limestone, grey or cream in colour. The Quantocks and the Brendon and Blackdown Hills are composed of hard red sandstone which provides another perfect building material, rough-hewn for house and cottage walls and easily dressed and carved to decorate churches. Villages in The Levels are built from the local blue lias, a durable stone which turns white with age.

In the Exmoor valleys where stone was not available, the rounded outlines of cottage walls betray the use of cob. But even the remotest village usually has a splendid church built with the profits from the wool trade which flourished during the 14th and 15th centuries. Wonderful towers supported by stepped and pinnacled buttresses, rising to battlements and fountains of crocketed pinnacles, grace the countryside. Inside, the roofs are magnificently timbered, often ornamented with bosses and supported by skilfully carved angels.

Other industries also brought prosperity. In the Mendips lead was possibly mined before the Romans came in AD 49 and the mining of iron and other minerals continued until the closure of the last mine near Priddy in 1908. But Somerset was always predominantly a farming county and still is today. The most fertile area is the Vale of Taunton, sheltered by the Quantocks to the north, the Brendons to the north-west and the Blackdowns to the south. From the hills you can look down on this lovely vale dotted with small towns, scattered villages and apple orchards. There is rich land also to the south and east. This is a world of cider and cream!

The lush grasslands of The Levels were once a huge freshwater swamp. Now drained by a network of ditches known as rhynes they provide some of the finest grazing land in England. The first settlements were made on islands of higher ground and the ruins of Muchelney Abbey, isolated on their low hill, still recall the remote atmosphere of those early days. Riverside paths and ancient drove ways, rich in rare plants and wildlife, lead deep into these unique wetlands.

Wildlife flourishes on the Somerset hills and Exmoor and the Quantocks are famous for their ponies and herds of red deer. Footpaths follow the crests of the hills giving glorious views south over Dartmoor and north over the Bristol Channel to the coast of Wales. Inspired by the Quantock countryside, Wordsworth and his friend Coleridge planned *The Lyrical Ballads*, a small book of romantic verse which was to revolutionise English poetry.

Romance, history and legend are so closely linked in Somerset that it is sometimes impossible to disentangle them. Everywhere you hear tales of Arthur and his fabled Camelot. The tiny village of South Cadbury nestles at the foot of a great hill fort whose ramparts guarded the headquarters of a 5th century warrior chieftain. Was this Arthur? Can the tradition that Christ accompanied his uncle Nicodemus on a trading expedition to Priddy be true? History records that King Alfred sought refuge from the Danes on the Isle of Athelney and while he was there he planned to regain Wessex. But did he really burn the cakes?

For this book I have chosen villages throughout the whole county in order to reveal as much as possible of Somerset's wonderfully varied countryside. All the walks are circular and range in length from 4 to 7½ miles. They are accompanied by simple sketch maps designed to guide you to the starting point and give an overall picture of the route. For more detailed information arm yourself with the relevant Ordnance Survey Landranger map noted in the introduction to each walk. Exmoor is covered by the Ordnance Survey Leisure map 9 at 1:25 000. Explorer maps also at 1: 25 000 have replaced Pathfinders. Places where food and drink can be obtained are given together with telephone numbers so that opening times can be checked. Car parking locations are indicated for each walk. But if they are full, or for some reason unusable, we are asked to respect the villagers' way of life. Please park carefully so as not to cause an obstruction.

Finally, I wish you many happy hours on foot in Somerset. I have very much enjoyed writing this book and I hope you will enjoy using it.

Anne-Marie Edwards

SELWORTHY

Length: 4 or 5 miles

Getting there: Selworthy is near the Exmoor coast, 4½ miles west of Minehead. Turn off the A39 following the sign 'Selworthy only'.	**Parking:** Drive uphill through the village. The road bends right, to the church on the left and the car park on the right. If this is full continue straight on for 75 yards to the overflow car park on the left.	**Map:** OS Landranger 181 Minehead & Brendon Hills (GR 920468).

No calendar of Somerset scenes would be complete without a picture of Selworthy! This delightful village, with its wealth of thatched cottages built of warm red stone sometimes colour-washed a deep cream, is a favourite with all visitors to Exmoor. But it remains tranquil and unspoilt. The church, coated white to protect its stonework, stands high on a south-facing hillside. From the porch you have a magnificent view over the Vale of Porlock to Exmoor's highest hill, Dunkery Beacon. Inside there is much to admire, including the splendid Perpendicular south aisle with its slender

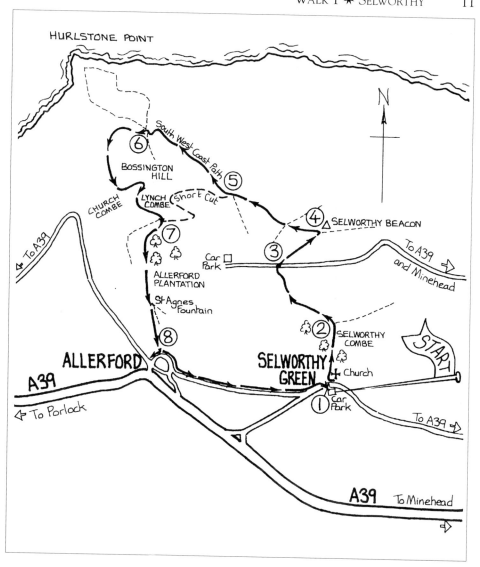

wreathed pillars and fine waggon roof. Below the church is a 13th century tithe barn. Originally the village was part of the 12,000 acre Holnicote estate owned by the Acland family but in 1944 Sir Richard Acland gave the estate to the National Trust.

Above the wooded hillsides sheltering the village, the coastal hills rise to their highest point at Selworthy Beacon, giving marvellous sea views. The walk follows tree-shaded paths up Selworthy Combe then crosses open moorland to the Beacon. You then head north-west along part of the

South West Coast Path towards the coast above Hurlstone Point. There is now a choice of routes. You can either continue round Bossington Hill along a dramatic cliff path or take an easier route down Lynch Combe. The two routes meet at the gate into Allerford Plantation. Woodland paths descend to Allerford village via St Agnes Fountain and a quiet track leads back to Selworthy.

THE WALK

❶ Walk past the church on your right and go through the small wooden gate to see Selworthy Green. The thatched cottages in their colourful gardens appear centuries old but most were rebuilt in 1828 by Sir Thomas Dyke Acland to provide comfortable homes for retired servants. Retrace your steps through the small gate and turn left, signed Selworthy Beacon. The track leads through a gate then becomes a beautiful path climbing through oak and beech woods with a stream tumbling down a ravine on the left.

❷ When the path divides bear left past a wooden barrier signed Selworthy Beacon. The path crosses the stream then continues to climb beside a smaller stream. At the top of the hill the path bears left with pines on the left, and open moorland on the right,

before curving a little right to meet a road.

❸ Cross the road and follow the moorland path bearing half-right to the stone cairn and trig. point on Selworthy Beacon. From here you enjoy wonderful views, north over the Bristol Channel to the hills of Wales, south and west over Exmoor, and east to the Brendons.

❹ Take the track that runs in front of the cairn and trig. point to leave them on your right and head west along the crest of the hill. Shortly the South West Coast Path joins your way from the right. Continue ahead as splendid cliff and sea views unfold before you. If you prefer to avoid the cliff path turn left, following the sign for the bridleway to Lynch, descend Lynch Combe and rejoin the longer walk at ❼, the gate into Allerford Plantation.

❺ For the longer walk keep ahead towards Hurlstone Point, following the sign 'Coast Path Bossington'. Now for some careful navigation! The path dips to a sign 'Coast Path Porlock'. Turn left following this sign and continue downhill for about 40 yards past a path on the left to meet a crosstrack. Turn left along a narrow cliffside path that keeps its height.

❻ The path curves round the seaward side of Bossington Hill giving spectacular views over Porlock Bay before winding round Church Combe, entering woodland and leading down to a crosstrack at Allerford Plantation.

❼ Ignore the signs on the right and go through the small wooden gate on the left by a sign for St Agnes Fountain, Allerford and Bossington. The path descends through the woods to crossing tracks in front of St Agnes Fountain, a small stream which rises out of the hillside to fall attractively over rust-coloured rocks into a stone basin. Just past the fountain you will see three paths. Take the lowest path on the right leading downhill for Allerford. Go through two wooden gates then walk over the field ahead to cross a stile by a gate to a lane.

❽ Your way is left here but make a detour to see Allerford by turning right for a few yards. Cross the cobbled packhorse bridge

> **PLACES of INTEREST**
>
> **Allerford Museum** (also known as the **West Somerset Rural Life Museum**) offers a fascinating recreation of rural life including a fully equipped Victorian kitchen and schoolroom. Riverside garden picnic area. Open Good Friday to October, weekdays 10.30 am to 1 pm and 2 pm to 4.30 pm; Saturday afternoons only and Sunday afternoons during school holidays. Telephone: 01643 862529.

and look back to see the charming picture made by the bridge over the stream and the old red stone house beyond. Retrace your steps and continue up the lane past your previous footpath on the left. When the lane bends right keep straight on along a

Selworthy Church.

narrow high-hedged track. Follow this for about a mile along the hillside then through a farmyard to meet the road in Selworthy village. Turn left past the tithe barn on the right and the gate to Selworthy Green on the left and turn right to the car park.

Looking towards Dunkery Beacon from Selworthy Church.

WINSFORD

Length: 4 or 6 miles

Getting there: Winsford is situated in the heart of Exmoor National Park. The best approach is via the A396 which runs south from Dunster on the coast towards Dulverton. Turn for Winsford about 4 miles south of Wheddon Cross.

Parking: Drive into Winsford and leave your car in the large parking area opposite the service station.

Map: OS Landranger 181 Minehead & Brendon Hills (GR 906349).

Winsford, deep in a densely-wooded valley, is many people's favourite Exmoor village. Little seems to have changed since the naturalist W. H. Hudson described the village in *Afoot in England* as 'second to no English village in beauty; with its hoary church tower, its great trees, its old stone, thatched cottages draped in ivy and vine, its soothing sound of running waters.' Here the Winn Brook meets the Exe, crossed by no fewer than eight bridges, two of which are narrow cobbled ways for packhorses.

The eminent statesman, Ernest Bevin, Minister of Labour during the Second World War, was born in Winsford in 1881. The house, close to the thatched Royal

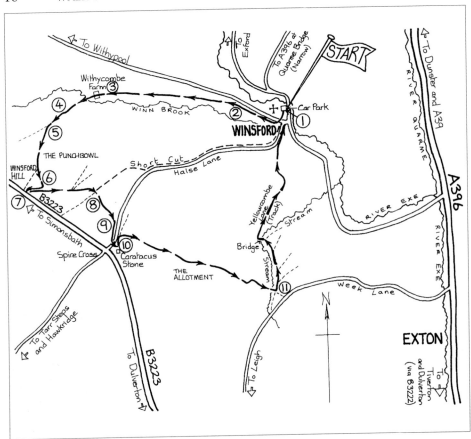

Oak Inn, is marked by a plaque. In March 1981 an oak tree was planted in the south-eastern corner of the village playing field by the respected trade union leader Jack Jones CH to commemorate the centenary of the birth of Ernest Bevin.

History and scenery combine to make this a fascinating walk. Meadow paths along the valley of the Winn lead to a striking natural amphitheatre with sides 200 feet deep known as the Punchbowl. Our path climbs round the rim of the Punchbowl and makes a detour to the top of Winsford Hill, giving wonderful views.

The shorter walk then takes moorland paths and lanes back to the village. The longer route leads to the sixth century Caratacus Stone, before crossing moorland

FOOD and DRINK

The picturesque Royal Oak Inn serves excellent meals in the bar and restaurant. Families are welcome. Telephone: 01643 851455. The Bridge Cottage Tea Rooms in the centre of the village serves coffee, snacks, sandwiches and cream teas. Open Easter to October, 10.30 am to 5.30 pm except Wednesday when it is 12.00 to 5.30 pm. Telephone: 01643 851362.

and descending through pinewoods to return to Winsford along an old packhorse track.

THE WALK

❶ Leave Bridge Cottage tea rooms on your right and turn right along the Withypool Road. Cross the footbridge and continue up the road past the church on the right.

❷ About 50 yards past the last house turn left through a gate following the sign 'footpath to Winsford Hill via Punchbowl'. Follow the grassy path ahead which bears right over a stile. Continue to cross the next stile and keep ahead with a hedge on your left. After crossing the next stile you follow a narrow path through a gate and along the foot of a meadow. The Winn Brook runs along the valley on your left. Keep ahead through a series of gates and across meadows until, after crossing a stream and going through a gate, you see two gates over the meadow ahead. Bear a little right to go through the right-hand gate and keep straight on with a hedge on the left – to meet a metalled track which leads down to the buildings of Withycombe Farm.

❸ Follow the track downhill to pass the farm buildings. The track bears left over the

The packhorse bridge over the Winn Brook at Winsford.

PLACES of INTEREST

Tarr Steps are about 4½ miles south-west of Winsford. The origins of this famous clapper bridge over the river Barle are unknown but it may be medieval or even prehistoric.

Winn then turns sharp right and becomes a stony way leading uphill through the left-hand of the two gates ahead. Now a path, our way bears right and begins to climb up the right-hand edge of the Punchbowl with a hedge on the right.

❹ As you near the top look carefully for a farm gate on the right marked with a blue bridleway square. Go through the gate and, bearing left, continue uphill with the hedge now on your left to go through another gate to the open moor.

❺ Follow the grassy path up the moor, ignoring all paths on the right. The path curves left round the rim of the Punchbowl to a crosspath.

❻ Turn right for about 300 yards to enjoy the view from the top of Winsford Hill beside the B3223. Close by are the Wambarrows, three burial mounds dating from the Bronze Age.

❼ Retrace your steps and keep straight ahead due east. When the path divides continue due east along the right-hand path to meet another crosstrack.

❽ For the shorter walk turn left over the moor to join Halse Lane. Bear left to follow the lane back to Winsford. For the longer

walk go straight over the crosstrack and continue, to meet Halse Lane further south just to the right of a house named 'Folly'.

❾ To see the Caratacus Stone turn right up the lane to meet the B3223 at Spire Cross. About 100 yards east from there you will see the slate roof of the shelter protecting the stone (GR 889335).

❿ Retrace your steps down Halse Lane for about 300 yards and look for a small wooden signpost on the right indicating a bridleway to Winsford. Follow this through a gate to continue along a wide moorland path that crosses the Allotment, an open expanse of moorland. The path descends to a small wooden gate. Go through and bear left, then right round the field (ignore gates on the left) to a signpost.

⓫ Turn left for Winsford through a gate into a pine wood and follow the left-hand of the two paths ahead, which drops steeply at first with a stream on the left. When the path divides take the left-hand narrower path, closer to the stream, and continue downhill to meet a wider track. At the next division take the left-hand path again. At all bridleway signs follow the path closest to the stream. At the bridleway sign pointing back the way you came marked 'Summerway', bear left to cross the stream by a wooden footbridge. The path turns left to a stile. Cross the stile and turn right to follow Yellowcombe Lane. In the days of packhorses this was the main route from Dulverton to Winsford. Meet Halse Lane near the village and turn right to return to your car.

LUCCOMBE

Length: 5½ or 7½ miles

Getting there: Luccombe is in the Exmoor National Park about 1½ miles south of the A39, between Porlock and Minehead.	Parking: From the A39 follow the sign for the village and at the T-junction turn left. After a few yards turn left into the parking area by the green.	Map: OS Landranger 181 Minehead & Brendon Hills (GR 912446).

You will find this enchanting village at the end of a narrow lane, tucked in a hollow at the foot of Dunkery Beacon, Exmoor's highest hill. 'Luccombe' probably means 'Lufa's valley', but there is a possibility it could mean 'the valley where courting was done' and no one could wish for more secluded and romantic surroundings! It is a tiny place composed mainly of thatched cottages, colour-washed deep cream with deep-set windows and massive chimneys. Some date from the 17th century, others are medieval in origin. A small stream overhung with flowers runs beside the village street. The nave and south aisle of the surprisingly large church of St Mary the

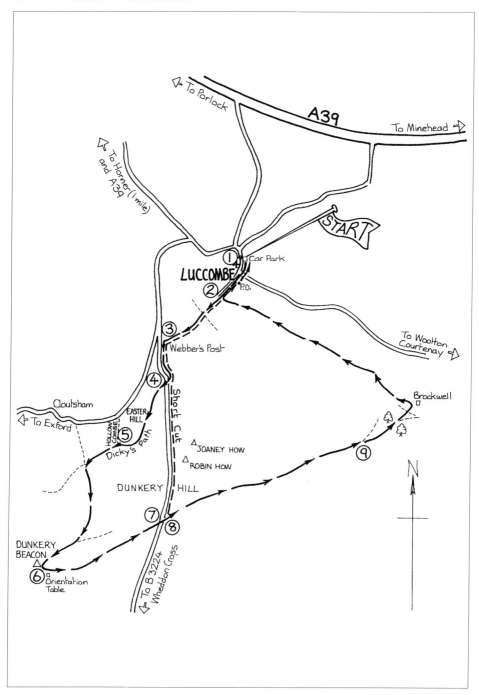

FOOD and DRINK

Some supplies can be purchased at the village shop in Luccombe. There are tea rooms in Horner, a nearby village. Porlock and Minehead are within easy reach.

Virgin have beautiful waggon roofs with elaborately carved oak ribs and painted wooden bosses. The pulpit is Jacobean and fragments of medieval glass are preserved in the windows.

Luccombe makes an ideal starting point for this dramatic walk which takes woodland and moorland paths to the top of Dunkery Beacon. From the summit, 1,750 feet above sea level, it is said you can see over 15 counties! The walk follows the crest of Dunkery Hill and then you can either return to Luccombe by the shorter route or take the path which crosses the moors to descend into the Vale of Porlock at Brockwell before returning to the village through the pine woods of Luccombe plantation.

THE WALK
❶ From the parking area turn left to walk up the village street, leaving the green on your left. Turn right in front of 'Ketnors', the thatched post office and shop. Continue along Stoney Street past the church on the right. Two of the cottages were originally medieval longhouses, housing the animals on the lower floor and the family in the hall above. Keep straight ahead up a track and through a gate.

❷ Follow the track as it climbs through mixed woodland of oak, beech and pine. All the way you are accompanied by a stream tumbling over the stones in a series of miniature waterfalls. Go over a crosstrack following the sign for Webber's Post. Continue up a more open path to meet a moorland road near the car park and picnic area at Webber's Post.

❸ Turn left to walk up the road for about ¼ mile. Shortly after a sharp left bend look carefully for a small wooden footpath sign on the right for Dicky's Path. (It may be partly obscured by bushes.) The sign indicates a narrow path bearing away from the road half-left across the moor. Ignore the path parallel with the road.

❹ Follow Dicky's Path as it curves round Easter Hill, then dips a little to bear right through the trees at the head of Hollow Combe. Beyond the ancient oaks clinging to the sides of the combe you look north at a typical Exmoor scene, a patchwork of green fields, heather-covered hills and deep wooded valleys.

❺ When the path divides take the left-hand path which rises gently to a crosspath. On the right the path drops steeply in the direction of Cloutsham, the farm on the hillside across the valley. Leave Dicky's Path and turn left to continue uphill aiming to the left of the summit. Join a clearer path and turn right to the cairn on top of Dunkery Beacon. Panoramic views in all directions are your reward and there is an orientation table to help you identify places as far away as Bodmin Moor, the Black Mountains and even the Malvern Hills! A plaque on the east side of the cairn gives details of the gift of the hill to the National Trust.

PLACES of INTEREST

A visit to Dunster, 2 miles east of Minehead, with its wealth of medieval buildings and impressive hilltop castle is a must! **Dunster Castle** (NT) is open 22nd March to 1st October (closed Thursday and Friday) 11 am to 5 pm; 4th October to 2nd November 11 am to 4 pm. For details telephone: 01643 821314.

❻ With your back to the plaque, leave the orientation table on your right and follow the white path heading east (with a touch of north) along the top of Dunkery Hill for about 1 mile. Go past a barrier to the moorland road you met earlier in the walk down at Webber's Post.

❼ For the shorter walk, turn left down the road to Webber's Post, then turn right to retrace your steps downhill to Luccombe.

❽ For the longer walk, cross straight over the road following the small wooden sign for Brockwell. Follow the white path ahead which crosses the moor below two prehistoric burial mounds, Robin How and Joaney How. Continue for over a mile, ignoring all paths on the left. The path begins to descend and bear a little left. After a steeper descent the path divides just before a wood.

❾ Take the right-hand path to walk

Dunkery Beacon, at 1,750 ft above sea level, the highest point on Exmoor.

Looking north from Dunkery Beacon.

through the wood. Keep following the Brockwell signs straight ahead. When the path divides take the left-hand path, go over a crosstrack and continue to a lane in the tiny hamlet of Brockwell. Turn left and keep ahead following the sign 'Bridleway Luccombe'. The track bears slightly right and becomes a wide way between high hedges signed for Horner, a small village about a mile west of Luccombe. Keep to this track as it winds through woods and crosses open hillsides, ignoring all paths on the left. Finally the track runs through the pines of Luccombe plantation and goes through a gate and across a bridge to rejoin your earlier path at the approach to the village. Turn right to retrace your steps down Stoney Street and turn left for the car park.

WALK 4

CORFE

Length: 4 miles

Getting there: Corfe is a small village 3 miles south of Taunton. It lies beside the B3170 which runs from Taunton south to meet the A303.

Parking: In the car park in Mill Lane at the north side of the church. Turn by the War Memorial and the car park is on the right.

Map: OS Landranger 193 Taunton & Lyme Regis (GR 233198).

Although lying either side of a busy road, Corfe has the peaceful atmosphere of a well cared for and much loved village. It is beautifully situated in the Vale of Taunton Deane, in the heart of Somerset's cream and cider country. Just south of the village rise the wooded slopes of the Blackdown Hills carved by streams into deep combes. Corfe's little neo-Norman church dedicated to St Nicholas stands in an idyllic spot, overlooking the valley of the Broughton Brook. The font has been preserved from the earlier church and has finely carved interlocking arches. Many

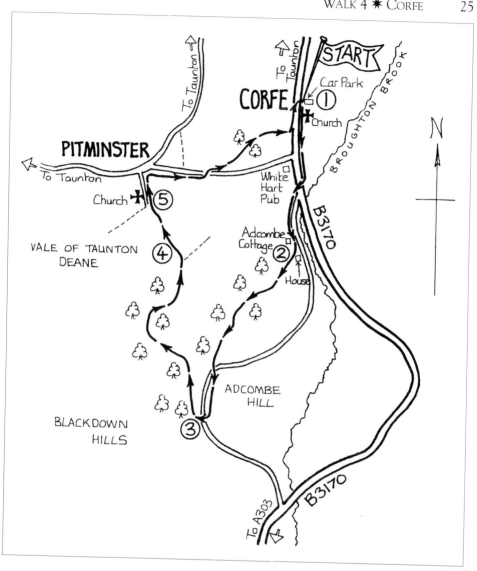

attractive houses line the village street including a delightful row of thatched cottages set behind neat lawns.

This exciting walk explores two contrasting worlds: the Vale, with its small, thickly-hedged meadows and the Blackdown Hills, clothed with ancient woodlands. From Corfe your path leads to the crest of Adcombe Hill, from where you can look north over the whole extent of the Vale to the Quantock Hills, west to the fringes of Exmoor and east to the great plain of the Somerset Levels. Woodland paths follow the crest of the Blackdowns before the route descends into the Vale to visit the secluded village of Pitminster and return to Corfe.

THE WALK

❶ From the car park walk past the War Memorial and turn left along the village street. Pass the White Hart pub on the right and continue along the footway. Turn right to follow Adcombe Lane. The lane leads along the valley past a footpath sign on the right.

❷ Just past Adcombe Cottage turn right up the next drive to walk past a house close on the left. (Although unsigned at the time

---

FOOD and DRINK

The White Hart in Corfe serves good meals and ales. You can enjoy these on the terrace with a view of the Blackdowns. Telephone: 01823 421388.

---

of writing this is a public right of way.) Keep ahead to go through a gate and follow the stony track which winds uphill through oak woods. Go through another gate and continue uphill. Already, as you gain height, you will be rewarded by lovely views of folded hills and hidden valleys. The track widens as another way joins from the right. Keep to the main track past a ruined cottage on the left to meet the corner of a

The wooded Blackdown Hills.

lane. Continue up the lane as it climbs gently over the top of Adcombe Hill.

❸ After about ¼ mile turn right, following the bridleway sign through a wooden gate to enter woods owned by the Woodland Trust. A wide terraced path now leads along the top of the hillside with glimpses of fields through a fringe of trees on the right. When the path forks keep straight ahead along the right-hand path. On the left the hillside drops steeply through tangled woods of oak, beech, birch and ash. Many of the nearer trees have been pollarded in the past to fire the lime kilns once numerous in this area. Both calamine and limestone were once quarried in these hills. Now the woods, bright with wild flowers, provide a quiet haven for deer. The path curves through the woods for over a mile before descending between thick hedges. The way becomes grassy as it bears a little left, leaving a track and house on the right. The spire of Pitminster church is now directly ahead.

❹ The track ceases before a gate and stile. Cross the stile and turn left with a hedge on the left and continue to a footpath sign on the left. Bear half-left now diagonally across the field keeping the spire of the church directly ahead. A few yards before the far left-hand corner of the field are two stiles and a small wooden bridge. Cross these and continue towards the spire to cross more stiles and another small bridge. Keep ahead, with the hedge on the right, and go through a gate to a lane to the left of Pitminster church. Turn right. Pitminster church is

---

PLACES of INTEREST

Sheppy's Farmhouse Cider, Bradford-on-Tone, is about 4 miles north-west of Corfe. Enjoy local draught and bottled cider, rural life museum, shop, farm trails and tours. Refreshments. Open Easter to Christmas, Monday to Saturday 8.30 am to 7 pm; Sunday 12 noon to 2 pm. Winter (closing at 6 pm) shop only. Telephone: 01823 461233.

Widcombe Wildlife and Country Park, about 4 miles south of Corfe is a 20 acre park with tropical birds and small animals, a shop and cafe. Open April to October daily from 10.30 am to 5. 30 pm. Telephone: 01823 421268.

---

well worth a visit. It houses fine monuments to the Colles family who bought the neighbouring Taunton Priory estate after the dissolution of the monasteries.

❺ Pass the church on the left and follow the lane through the village to a T-junction. Turn right and after a few yards turn right again, signed Corfe, and follow the lane past a footpath sign on the left. Pass Fly Boat Farm and turn left at the next footpath sign to cross the stile. Turn immediately right and cross the stile ahead. The right of way now bears a little left to cross the next field between two magnificent oak trees, aiming for the left-hand corner of a small belt of woodland. (You may prefer to walk round the field.) The path becomes clear as it passes a little pond on the right and continues over the next field. When you reach the hedge bear right to cross a stile into Corfe village street. Turn left to walk back to the church and your car.

BROMPTON REGIS

Length: 5½ miles

Getting there: Brompton Regis lies in the Brendon Hills within the southern boundary of the Exmoor National Park. Approaching from the west, turn for the village off the A396 between Tiverton and Dunster. From the east take the B3224, turn left along the B3190, then turn right following the sign for Brompton Regis.

Parking: At the top end of the village turn down Knightstone Mead, pass the side of the village hall and turn immediately left into the parking area.

Map: OS Landranger 181 Minehead & Brendon Hills (GR 949313).

The Brendon Hills east of the Exe valley do not seem to receive as much attention as other areas in the National Park but they include a great deal of lovely scenery; some of the most attractive surrounds Brompton Regis, a spacious village standing high on a southern slope of the hills. Once a busy market town, it is now a quiet place, its narrow streets lined with houses built of multi-coloured stone. The church of St Mary the Virgin has a 13th century tower and a beautifully arcaded north aisle dating from the late 15th century. Known locally as 'Kingsbrompton', the royal addition to

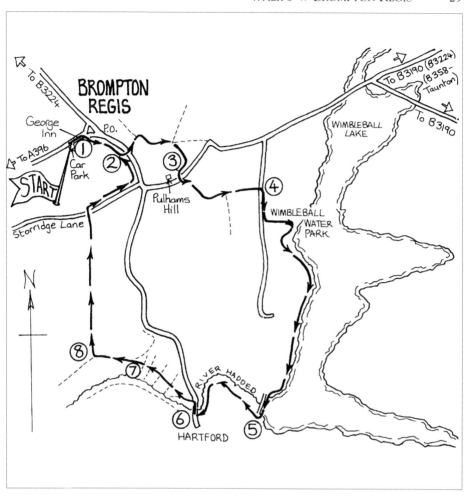

the village name dates from the time of William the Conqueror who seized the manor from Gytha, mother of King Harold, after the Battle of Hastings.

In 1974, Southern Water dammed the headwaters of the River Haddeo to create Wimbleball reservoir. It is now a delightful lake covering 374 acres, with wooded shores and a background of rounded hills. From the village we take field paths to the lake and follow the shore south to cross the dam, enjoying splendid views east over the lake, and west along the valley of the Haddeo. The route follows the riverside to Hartford, before climbing through Hartford Wood and returning to the village.

THE WALK
❶ From the parking area return to the road and turn right past the village hall and the George Inn. Just past the inn turn right through an iron gate and follow a narrow

path running downhill past the church to meet a lane. Walk down the lane past the post office.

❷ Just before the de-restriction signs turn left along a footpath, designated 'R.U.P.P.' (road used as public footpath). Cross a wooden footbridge and bear right to a T-junction. Turn right and continue to another T-junction where you turn right to a road.

❸ Turn right down the road for about 200 yards to a house on the left. Before the wall of the house, look for a footpath marked by an inconspicuous sign on the left for Wimbleball. Turn left along a narrow path and cross two stiles to a field. Bear right and walk down the side of the field, with a hedge on the right. When the hedge ends, descend the steep bank on the right then bear left to resume your former heading and cross a footbridge. Go through a gate and walk up the field ahead, the hedge on the right. Continue uphill through a gateway and up the next field, to go through a gate to a lane.

❹ Bear right along the lane and turn left through the entrance to Wimbleball Lake Water Park. Keep straight ahead past the kiosk on the left to the shore of Wimbleball Lake and turn right, signed Lakeside Walk. Through a small gate the path leads across wildflower meadows. After a second gate, cross the lane to the sailing club, go up the steps and follow the path ahead as it skirts the club and crosses more meadows before running through Eastern Wood. The path curves right over a meadow to reveal the dam in the valley. Walk down to a lane, bear right over a stile, then turn left to walk across the dam.

❺ On the other side turn right down a concrete road. Continue downhill, ignoring all side paths, to go through a gate signed 'Lady Harriet's Drive'. This commemorates the bravery of Lady Harriet Acland. During the American War of Independence her husband, Major Acland, was wounded at the battle of Saratoga in 1777, and taken prisoner. Lady Harriet crossed the Hudson river to nurse him in the enemy camp and the Major was able to return home. The path now crosses a meadow and curves left. Look for a sign on the left 'Bridleway to Bury'. (Ignore the path 'avoiding the houses'.) Turn left beside the river to a wooden footbridge. Cross the bridge, bear left along the other side of the river and just past a house turn right through the gate of Hartford Mill. Walk up to a track with several signs.

❻ Turn right (no sign) for just a few yards and look for a narrow path leading uphill on the left signed ' Louisa Gate, Dulverton and Brompton Regis'. The path winds up into Hartford Woods. After about ¼ mile the path divides. Take the right-hand path uphill. (The path is waymarked at times with white squares on the trees.) This brings you to a crosstrack with a small wooden sign, 'permitted path', indicating

PLACES of INTEREST

Wimbleball Lake Water Park offers a wide variety of outdoor activities. For details contact the Ranger (telephone: 01398 371372) from April to October. The Gift and Tea Shop is open Easter to October, 11 am to 5 pm every day. Telephone: 01398 371257. For the Sailing Club telephone: 01278 652146. At **Pulhams Mill** you can buy furniture made at the mill in English hardwood and beautiful hand painted china. Open in summer Monday to Friday, 10 am to 6 pm (Saturday 5 pm). In winter it is usually open Monday to Saturday, 10 am to 5 pm but telephone 01398 371366 to confirm.

crosstrack. Keep straight on here still uphill for about 100 yards to go straight over yet another crosstrack (making four in all). Continue uphill to meet a crossing track which runs across the top of the hill with the woods on the left and a high embankment crowned with trees concealing fields on the right.

❼ Turn left and follow this track with the embankment on your right for about ¼ mile.

❽ Navigate carefully at this point! Look carefully for a break in the embankment with a track running through it. There is a

the grassy track straight ahead. Follow this for about 200 yards to another crosstrack. Bear right here, uphill, to the next

Wimbleball Lake.

The dam across the River Haddeo, with Wimbleball Lake in the background.

small wooden signpost on the right before the track but it may be obscured. Turn right to follow a tree-shaded path heading north. Keep a hedge on the left as the path leaves the woods to cross meadows and stiles and go through iron gates before descending through a final gate to Storridge Lane. Turn right down the lane to a junction, then bear left to return to Brompton Regis.

CROWCOMBE

Length: 6½ miles

Getting there: Crowcombe is about 10 miles north of Taunton. Turn for the village off the A358 Taunton to Minehead road.	**Parking:** In the car park opposite the church.	**Map:** OS Landranger 181 Minehead & Brendon Hills (GR 140367).

Crowcombe nestles at the foot of the steep western slopes of the Quantock Hills. It is a beautiful village built of local rose-coloured sandstone, surrounded by gardens and orchards which merge imperceptibly into the wooded hillsides. The 14th century tower of the church was once topped by an 80 foot spire. Struck by a thunderbolt in 1725, the tip of the spire can still be seen in the churchyard. Inside the church the Tudor bench ends are among the finest in Somerset. On one of the most delightful two men vigorously attack a double-headed dragon. By the car park is a rare survival, a Church House. Once used to bake bread and brew beer for 'Church Ales', annual festivities which provided funds for repairs, this venerable building is now the village

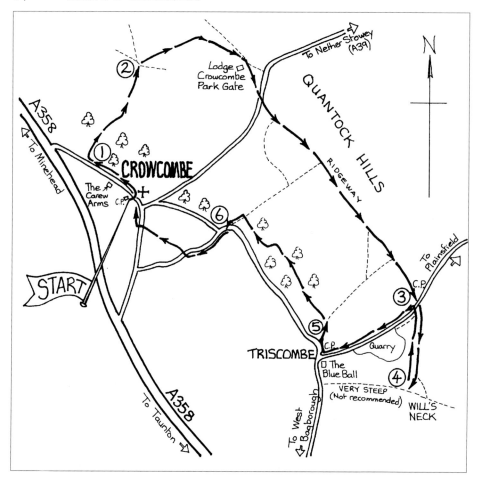

hall. The manor house, Crowcombe Court, was built for Thomas Carew in the early 18th century.

This superb walk follows a historic ridgeway along the crest of the hills to reach the highest point on the Quantocks, Will's Neck, 1,260 feet above sea level. The return route takes lower paths through oak and beech woods. The views throughout the walk are breathtaking and there is always the chance of spotting red deer on the moor.

THE WALK

❶ From the car park walk past the side of the Church House to the road and turn left to pass the church on the right. There is a fine view on the right of Crowcombe Court, now a retirement home. In medieval times Crowcombe had a market and as you continue down the road you pass the 13th century butter cross. Pass the Carew Arms on the left. The doors and windows are painted a rather startling blue which denotes a property still owned by the manor. Continue for about another 100 yards to a flight of stone steps on the right.

❷ Turn right up the steps signed for Crowcombe Park Gate. Follow the narrow path ahead to cross two stiles. After the second stile there is no clear path but keep straight on up the field to go through a gap in the embanked hedge and over a stile. Cross a track and climb the fence ahead. Again there is no clear path but bear slightly right up the field aiming for the corner of a fence to the left of a belt of woodland. Now walk straight on and as you gain height you will see an iron gate ahead. Cross the fence beside the gate to follow a beech-shaded path which climbs the hillside to a pair of gateposts facing open moorland.

❸ Ignore the path sharp right along the edge of the wood and follow the next path which curves a little right over a rise and meets another path. Bear right to follow the path along the hillside with the wood about 50 yards away on the right. When the path runs closer to the wood, cross the stile by a wooden gate and continue to a wide track. When the track divides take the right-hand track which leads past the lodge at Crowcombe Park Gate to a road. Cross, and take the wide path ahead with a wall, earth-filled and studded with trees (typical of the Quantocks) on your left. This ridgeway was

a Bronze Age trading route. Go through the gate by the National Trust sign and along the crest of Great Hill. When the path dips take the left hand of the two paths ahead and continue along the ridge to go through a gate and leave the National Trust land. Keep on for about ¼ mile to the top of the lane which leads down to Triscombe Quarry. There is a car park on the left.

❹ Cross the lane to the quarry and keep ahead for about 50 yards past a narrow unmarked path on the right. Turn right up the next path, which is signed and has a notice, 'no bikes or vehicles', and climb to the top of Will's Neck, taking the right-hand path at the division. You will be rewarded by magnificent views: west to the Brendon Hills and Exmoor, east over the Levels with the blue line of the Mendips beyond, north over the Severn Estuary to the coast of Wales and south over the vale of Taunton Deane to the Blackdown hills.

❺ Retrace your steps to the quarry road and turn left down the road to the Blue Ball pub at Triscombe. Pass the pub car park on the right and immediately after turn right up an unsigned lane. Continue for about 60 yards to the point where the lane curves left.

❻ Leave the lane and keep straight ahead following the blue arrow bridleway sign. Go through the gate into National Trust land and continue for about 30 yards to a post marked with a yellow arrow footpath sign. Leave the main track and bear left uphill with a tree-planted wall on your left. Keep to the narrow path through woods and along more open hillsides before descending through beech woods to go through a small wooden gate. Continue for about 200 yards to a post with a yellow footpath sign indicating a left turn. Turn left and follow the path downhill to a crosstrack. Turn left through a gate to pass farm buildings and go through another gate to a lane.

❼ Turn right along the lane past Little Quantock Farm and take the left hand lane a little further on. Continue for about ¼ mile to an iron gate on the right. (The footpath sign may be obscured.) Turn right over the fence beside the gate and keep ahead over the meadow to cross a stile. Continue with a hedge on your right, to go

through a small wooden gate which opens into the road in Crowcombe. Turn right to return to the car park.

PLACES of INTEREST

Crowcombe Church House is open June to September from Monday to Friday, 2.30 to 4.30 pm. **The West Somerset Railway** captures the great days of steam, running for 20 miles between Bishop's Lydeard and Minehead. Talking timetable: 01643 707650. Enquiries: 01643 704996. **Combe Sydenham Country Park** offers a splendid day out for all the family. Open March 1st to September 30th, Sunday to Friday 9 am to 5 pm. Telephone: 01984 656364. **Bee World and Animal Centre,** approx. 3 miles from Crowcombe, is open April 1st to October 31st, 10 am to 6 pm all week. Telephone: 01984 656545.

Crowcombe's 15th-century Church House, now the village hall.

EAST QUANTOXHEAD

Length: 6 miles

Getting there: East Quantoxhead is about 12 miles east of Minehead. Turn for the village off the A39 Bridgwater to Minehead road.	**Parking:** Drive into the village and turn left into the car park opposite the duckpond.	**Map:** OS Landranger 181 Minehead & Brendon Hills (GR 136437).

In 1797 William Wordsworth and his sister Dorothy rented Alfoxton Park, a large Georgian house high on the northernmost bluff of the Quantock Hills with a splendid view over Bridgwater Bay to the coast of Wales. Dorothy wrote to a friend: 'There is everything here; sea, woods wild as fancy ever painted, brooks clear and pebbly as in Cumberland, villages so romantic.' Among

the romantic villages that delighted her she must have included East Quantoxhead. Situated in the shadow of the hills only half a mile from the sea, the village presents an idyllic picture. Church, manor and thatched cottages cluster around a large pond complete with colourful tribes of ducks. After the Norman Conquest the village was granted to Ralph Pagnell and it

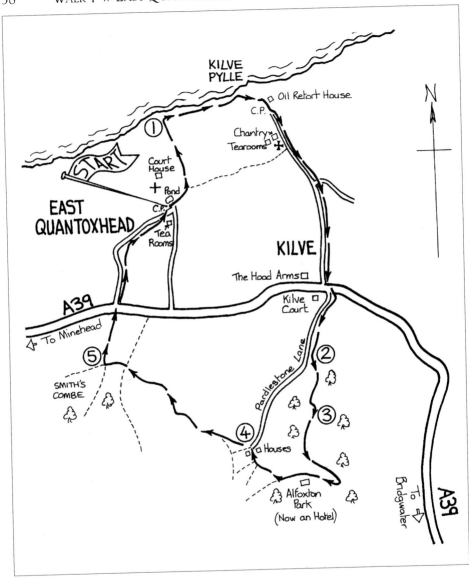

is still owned by his descendant, Sir Walter Fownes Luttrell who occupies the manor, Court House. The church close by dates from the 14th century and retains its medieval rood screen and 16th century carved bench ends.

From the village, the walk heads seawards and follows the coast path to Kilve Pylle, a small bay where the cliffs give way to a grassy inlet. Here smugglers once landed contraband. The route then turns inland through Kilve village and climbs to

FOOD and DRINK

There are tearooms in East Quantoxhead, clearly marked from the car park. The Chantry Tea Gardens, Chantry Cottage, close to the beach at Kilve offers cream teas, ices and hot soup. Bed and breakfast. Telephone: 01278 741457. The Hood Arms beside the A39 at Kilve is a 17th century coaching inn welcoming families and offering bar meals as well as a restaurant menu. Telephone: 01278 741210.

pass Alfoxton House. A moorland path with wide sea views joins a quiet lane to return to East Quantoxhead.

THE WALK

❶ Turn right from the car park, then left round the pond following the sign for the beach. Pass the thatched mill house and walk beside the stream with the gardens of Court House also on your left. Keep to the main track then turn left to follow the sign for the beach. Go through a gate and take the wide grassy track straight ahead. On the hillside on the left you have a fine view of Court House, a medieval manor much altered during the centuries. Through the next gate a sign directs you to the Coast Path.

❷ Bear right to follow the Coast Path along the clifftop. This is a wild and romantic place with the sheer cliffs and headlands of Bridgwater Bay rising to east and west. Below, the broken strands of flat shale-bearing rock reaching seawards from the foot of the cliffs are famous for their fossils. The path narrows to descend to Kilve Pylle where the grass running down to the beach makes an ideal place for a picnic. Continue the walk along the main path to cross a bridge and pass a tall brick building on the left. A panel explains that this is the remains of an oil retort house. In the mid 1920s attempts were made to extract oil from the shale but the process proved too costly and was soon abandoned. Follow the path as it bears right and becomes an asphalted lane passing a car park on the right. A little further are the ruins of a chantry founded in 1329 by Sir Simon de Furneaux. The chantry was destroyed, it is said, by a fire fuelled by kegs of smuggled brandy! The simple grey stone church close by dates from the 13th century.

Follow the lane through the village to the main road, the A39. Cross straight over and take Pardlestone Lane marked with a no-through-road sign. This very pretty way winds between banks of wild flowers past Kilve Court, a Georgian mansion. Continue up the lane to an iron gate on the left with a blue bridleway sign.

❸ Turn left through the gate and follow the path along the edge of a field with a wood on the left. The path bears right with a fence now on the left. When the fence gives way to a hedge continue for a few yards then turn left through a gate.

❹ Turn right and continue up the field with the hedge now on your right. Go through a high iron gate and follow the path which soon bears left and rises more steeply with a hedge on the right and a fence on the left. Continue through two more iron gates. The path curves left, hedge on right and descends to meet a good track by a bridleway sign. Turn right through an iron gate then right again beside a cattle grid to follow the drive to Alfoxton Park

The beautiful gardens at Court House.

Hotel. Here the Wordsworths entertained Coleridge and worked on poems to be included in their book *The Lyrical Ballads*. Wordsworth's statement in the Preface that ordinary people and everyday events were suitable themes for the poet was to cause a revolution in English verse.

Continue up the lane marked no-through-road which curves left to pass the YHA sign and Alfoxton Cottage. Keep to the lane as it drops steeply and becomes a rough stony track passing some cottages. Ignore a path on the left leading up the moor and descend to the next path on the left signed for Perry.

❺ Turn left to follow this delightful path, which runs along the edge of the moorland with green fields sloping towards the coast over the hedge on the right. The path dips and rises through wooded combes. Pass a signpost on the right for the A39 and keep on for Perry. Soon after the path descends into Smith's Combe to another signpost.

❻ Turn right signed for East Quantoxhead and continue over the grass with a stream on your left. The path leads through two gates to the A39. Cross over and follow the lane for East Quantoxhead. When you come to a footpath sign on the right you can cross the stile, bear left and cross another stile to rejoin the lane and so cut the corner, or you can follow the lane back to the village, bearing left to return to the car park.

HOLFORD

Length: 5½ miles

| Getting there: Holford lies just west of the A39 between Bridgwater and Minehead.

Parking: The car park is beside Holford Bowling Green. Turn off the | A39 past the front of the Plough Inn and follow the narrow lanes through the village, turn left at the T-junction then right by some thatched cottages following the car park sign. The car park is a few yards further on the left. | Map: OS Landranger 181 Minehead & Brendon Hills (GR 155411). |

The eastern slopes of the Quantock Hills, rising less steeply than those facing west, are threaded by beautifully wooded combes. Old world villages lie half-hidden in these deep valleys and one of the most delightful is Holford. Today the houses and cottages of the village slumber peacefully in their tranquil setting but during the 17th century cloth was woven here and there were two fulling mills by the stream. Copper was mined from the late 18th century and a large tannery was built nearby. The tiny church, standing among the meadows, has a curious saddle-back tower and you will find an ancient cross in the churchyard.

If you enjoy ancient oak woods and all the

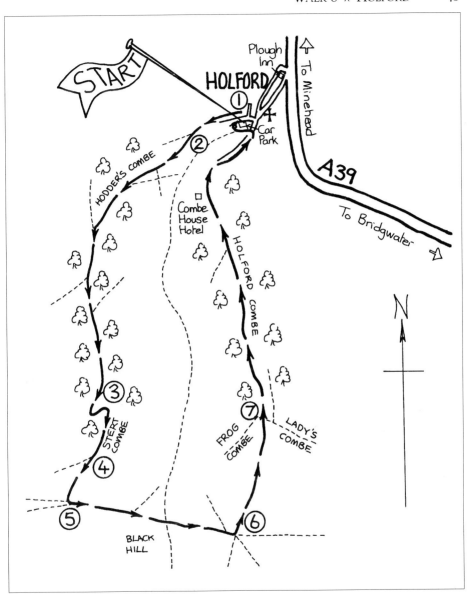

wildlife that they encourage do not miss this walk! The route explores two of the loveliest valleys in the Quantocks. We follow Hodder's or Butterfly Combe to the high moor giving glorious views to the sea before descending Holford Combe and returning to the village. If you are lucky you may spot the red deer which seek shelter in these dense woodlands.

THE WALK

❶ Several paths lead from the car park. With your back to the access road and the car park on your left you will see two tracks running parallel on your right between the car park and Holford Bowling Green. Take the right-hand track immediately to the left of the green. Pass houses to right and left, then follow the track as it leads into the beautiful woods of Hodder's Combe. The ground beneath the trees is carpeted with whortleberry bushes - best visited in July and August for their fruit!

❷ When the track divides take the left-hand path, which climbs gently between

FOOD and DRINK

The Plough Inn at Holford is well known for its excellent food and ales. Telephone: 01278 741232.

steep slopes with a stream on the right. The path hugs the bank of the stream then crosses open glades where the sunlight allows woodland flowers to flourish, including masses of bluebells in late spring and tall spikes of foxgloves in June. When the path narrows and divides take the left-hand path which bears away from the stream you have been following. Another stream now accompanies you on the left. Keep ahead past a joining path on the left.

Holford Church, with its curious saddle-back tower.

After about 300 yards cross the stream and continue to climb gently with the stream now on your right. Keep to the main path which now dips to cross the stream again before climbing the opposite bank. Ignore all side paths and keep to the main path as it begins to climb more steeply.

❸ The path curves a little right then more sharply left to lessen the gradient as it ascends the hillside. A final curve to the right and the path leaves the trees to bring you to the open moor.

❹ When the path divides keep ahead up the right-hand path with Stert Combe on your left to a crosspath.

❺ Turn left to follow the path over the high moor to enjoy a splendid view north over Bridgwater Bay and the islands of Flat Holm and Steep Holm. Beyond rise the blue shadows of the Welsh hills. After about 100 yards you join a wider track. Continue along this still heading east. Pass a track on the left and continue over the crosstrack on Black Hill. Keep ahead past another track on the left. The track dips then rises. From the top of the rise continue for about 200 yards to a point where several paths converge. (The distance from ❺ is about ¼ mile.)

❻ Turn left along a green path which heads north across the moor, then becomes stony and drops steeply beneath the gnarled and stunted oaks of Holford Combe to a stream. This is a particularly remote and secret place with Lady's Combe on the right and Frog Combe on the left.

❼ Bear left along a good track with the stream on your right. The stream is your guide for the rest of the walk. After crossing a tributary stream the path divides. Ignore the path on the left which runs steeply uphill and continue along the level right-hand path. The stream meanders first at one side of your path and then at the other. It does not matter which bank you follow - just choose the easiest way! Eventually you will find the better path runs to the right of the stream and becomes a metalled lane. After passing some cottages you will see Combe House Hotel on the left. Originally this was a major tannery complex and the hotel retains the giant iron water wheel of 1893 and other workings. Continue down the lane to a bridleway sign on the left. Turn left to cross the stream by a house, turn right when the paths divide and at the crosspath keep straight on down through the wood. At the foot of the hill turn right into the car park.

PLACES of INTEREST

At Nether Stowey is **Coleridge Cottage** (NT), home of the poet from 1797 to 1800. It is open March to September, Tuesday to Thursday and Sunday 2 pm to 5 pm. Telephone: 01278 732662.

STOKE ST GREGORY

Length: 4½ miles

Getting there: Stoke St Gregory stands on a ridge which runs north-east across the Somerset Levels about 6 miles east of Taunton. Approaching from the east turn for North Curry off the A378 and continue to Stoke St Gregory,	turning right for the centre of the village. Approaching from the north along the A361 turn for the village at Burrow Bridge. **Parking:** Drive through the square past the church and take the next	turning on the right into the church car park. Sunday mornings, park in the square. **Map:** OS Landranger 193 Taunton & Lyme Regis (GR 348272).

The charming village of Stoke St Gregory makes a perfect starting point for an exploration of the Somerset Levels. Whitewashed 18th century houses cluster round a small square overlooked by a fine church built in the form of a cross with a central octagonal tower dating from the

12th century. Above the south door is a 15th century Ham stone statue of St Gregory. Inside you will find a beautifully carved Jacobean pulpit and well-preserved Elizabethan bench ends. Stocks - with room for three! - stand in the churchyard.

From the village there are splendid

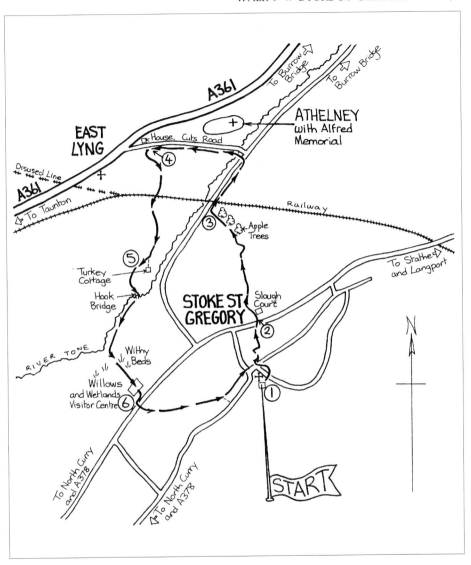

views west over Curry Moor and the river Tone. Here King Alfred sought refuge from the Danes on the Isle of Athelney – now just a small hill – which, at that time, was surrounded by marshes. It was in January, AD878, that the Danes overran King Alfred's kingdom, Wessex, forcing him to flee to Athelney. But Alfred was a fine strategist as well as a great commander. In March, while his men harried the Danes who were watching from the Poldens, Alfred rode secretly to 'Egbert's Stone' in the Forest of Selwood, east of Frome. Here he was joined by men from Somerset,

FOOD and DRINK

The Rose and Crown in Stoke St Gregory is a real country pub offering excellent meals and ales. Telephone: 01823 490296.

Hampshire and Wiltshire. He surprised the Danes by attacking from the east and defeated them at the battle of Ethandune (modern Edington). The treaty of Wedmore followed. The Danish king Guthrum and 30 of his thanes agreed to Christian baptism and Alfred allowed them to retreat to East Anglia and settle there. So, from a small island in the Somerset marshes, Alfred won back his kingdom and helped to save western civilisation. The walk follows in his footsteps.

The route then crosses Curry Moor and runs beside the Tone before visiting the fascinating Willows and Wetlands Visitor Centre at Meare Green Court. Meadow paths lead back to the village.

THE WALK

❶ From the car park, turn left into the lane and pass the church on the left. Opposite the pub turn right for a few yards then left up Church Close. Take the first turning on the right. Just past number 16 turn left to follow a narrow path to the right of a thick hedge. Cross a stile and continue with a hedge on the right. Ahead rises a conical hill, Burrow Mump, crowned with an unfinished church. King Alfred may have built a fort here as a look-out post. Cross a stile to a lane, and bear right for a few yards.

❷ Turn left up the track signed Slough Court to pass barns on the right. You come to a stile on the left leading into a field.

Before crossing this look right to see medieval Slough Court.

Cross the stile and bear right to go through a gate to the left of a bungalow. There is no clear path but keep straight ahead towards the corner of a wire fence. Across the field you will see a row of trees. Walk over the field aiming for a gate just to the right of the trees. Looking back, Stoke St Gregory church tower is directly in line. From the gate a wide drove leads to a rhyne, one of many drainage ditches criss-crossing the Levels. Turn right for a few yards then left over a bridge. Go through a gate and bear left for about 60 yards then turn right to follow a row of apple trees to a lane.

❸ Turn right and follow the lane over the level crossing. Turn left into Cuts Road, signed Lyng, and cross the bridge over the Tone. The small hill ahead is the Isle of Athelney, and just to the right of a farm stands the Alfred memorial. Follow Cuts Road until it begins to rise to pass a house on the right.

❹ Look carefully for a wooden gate on the left (unsigned). Turn left through the gate and bear right beside the grassy mound of a garden for a few yards to some wooden bars on the right. Cross these and turn left to continue with a hedged rhyne on the left. Cross a narrow bridge and continue over the railway. From the stile on the other side turn right to a wire fence, then bear left along a good track. Cross a bridge and continue until the track comes to another bridge leading to Turkey Cottage.

❺ Turn right before the bridge through a gate, then bear left to continue to the right of the rhyne. Cross stiles and sluice gates and turn left over Hook Bridge. Turn right over the stile and follow the bank of the Tone, with the river on the right, for around 200 yards. Over the grass on the left you will see a plank bridge leading to a gate and a path through the withy beds which becomes a white track winding uphill. Turn left to follow this over the ridge to the Willows and Wetlands Centre.

❻ From the Centre gate turn right along the road for a few yards then left up a sunken track to a stile. Cross and turn left to continue, the hedge on your left. When the hedge turns left bear a little right down the field to cross a wooden railed footbridge. Turn right to another bridge but do not cross. Bear left, with a hedge on the right, and continue over stiles. Cross a small close and keep straight on to the road. Turn right past Stoke St Gregory school to walk back to the church and car park.

The memorial to King Alfred on the tiny 'isle' of Athelney.

MUCHELNEY

Length: 5½ miles

Getting there: Muchelney is a small village in the Somerset Levels a mile south of Langport. The best approach is via the A372. Turn for Muchelney opposite the church in Huish Episcopi (on the western outskirts of Langport). Shortly after,	turn left again following the sign for Muchelney down the narrow lane that leads to the village. **Parking:** In the National Trust car park in Muchelney from April 1st to September 30th. Turn left in front of	the church and the car park is on the right. At other times park in front of the church. **Map:** OS Landranger 193 Taunton & Lyme Regis (GR 429248).

A vast plain of rich grassland watered by slow meandering rivers and drained by a network of ditches called rhynes forms the heart of Somerset. It is a unique, mysterious wetland with a fascinating history and a wealth of wildlife. Originally the whole area was a wilderness of swamps and marshes dotted with low islands settled by small isolated communities. If you would like to step back in time and enjoy the tranquillity of this very special part of Somerset, you must visit one of the most beautiful and least changed of the villages of the Levels, Muchelney.

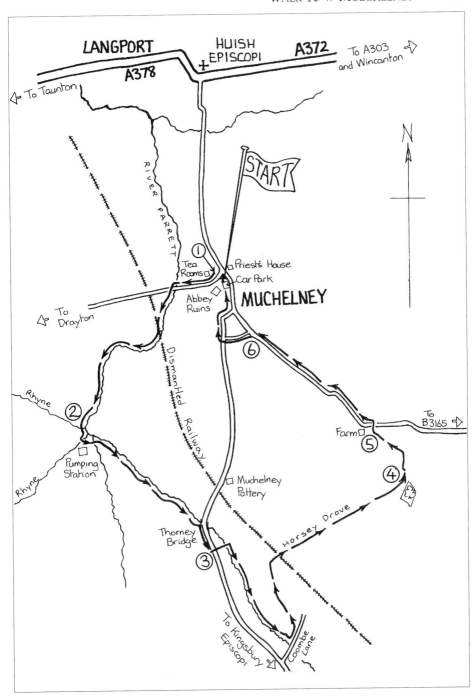

FOOD and DRINK

I can recommend the Abbey tea rooms housed in a
16th century barn. Everything is home-made and
among the delights on offer are freshly squeezed fruit
juices, a range of cakes, and pastries with comb honey
and clotted cream. Savouries include platters of
smoked trout and salmon. Painting courses are held
here and there is also a supper club. Telephone: 01485
253382.

A Benedictine Abbey was founded here
in the 9th century. The monks drained and
cultivated the land and cared for travellers,
children and the sick. After the dissolution
the Abbey crumbled into decay but the
Abbot's lodging remains almost perfect
with kitchen, hall and fine parlour. The
south wall of the cloisters, two storeys high,
also survives. Close to the site of the Abbey
stands the church built by the monks for
the villagers in the 15th century. The
waggon roof is decorated with angels in
low-cut Tudor costumes waving texts and
on either side of the north porch are two
grotesque heads known as 'hunky punks'
typical of this part of Somerset. A charming
thatched house built for the priest in 1308
stands opposite. He lived well as the monks
were obliged to provide him with bread,
fish, eggs and two gallons of best ale every
day except Sundays and Tuesdays when he
had meat!

There is much more to enjoy in
Muchelney. The houses and cottages are
built of the local stone, blue lias, the light
colour contrasting with the rich gold Ham
stone used to frame windows and doors. A
tiny white-washed toll house greets you as
you enter the village and the rebuilt
Almonry House features a small stone
figure of a monk above the door.

Do this walk in summer if you can to
enjoy the wild flowers beside the rhynes
and in the meadows. The route follows the
bank of the River Parrett with wide views
over the plain punctuated by the tall
church towers of scattered villages. After
visiting the picturesque village of Thorney
Bridge an old drove road leads back to
Muchelney. Take your binoculars! Among
the wildlife you are likely to see are herons,
kingfishers, rare birds of prey and deer.

THE WALK

❶ Start from the church. Turn left round
the church following the lane signed
Drayton, with the Tea Rooms on the right.
Pass the Abbey ruins and follow the lane to
Westover Bridge. Cross the bridge and turn
left following the footpath sign for Thorney
Bridge. Follow the bank of the River
Parrett, bearing right before the supports for
a bridge which once carried a railway over
the river. After about ¼ mile you will see a
modern pumping station on the opposite
bank.

❷ About 30 yards past the pumping
station turn left over two bridges. The track
bears left past the front of the pumping

PLACES of INTEREST

Muchelney Abbey (English Heritage) is open daily 10
am to 6 pm (closed from 1 pm to 2 pm) from April 1st to
September 30th. Telephone: 01179 750700. The
Priest's House (NT) is open from the same dates,
Sunday and Monday 2 pm to 5 pm Telephone: 01458
252621. **Muchelney Pottery** is a mile south of the
village at Thorney. Here you can watch the craftsmen
at work. The pottery shop is open all year Monday to
Friday, 9 am to 1 pm and 2 pm to 5 pm; Saturday 9 am
to 1 pm. Telephone: 01458 250324.

station, over a bridge, and then bears a few yards to the left before turning right over a narrow wooden-railed bridge and a stile. Bear right to follow the river bank once more with the river on your left. You come to a road at Thorney Bridge. Turn right to walk through the village.

❸ Look for a sign, 'Private drive, footpath only', on the left in front of Mill House. (There is a less obvious footpath sign for Gawbridge.) Turn left to walk past the mill, over a narrow iron-railed bridge, and turn right to follow the river bank, the river now on your right. Continue to a stile leading

into Coombe Lane beside Coombe Bridge. Turn left along the lane and after about 200 yards bear left along a track running to the right of a rhyne to meet Horsey Drove. Bear right to follow the drove for almost a mile.

❹ Pass a small wood on the right and bear left through a gate to cross a field with a rhyne on the right. As you reach the far corner keep straight on along a narrow path through the bushes and over a stile. The path bears left and becomes more open and grassy as it runs under trees.

❺ Before you reach a farm, turn right over

A picnic by the River Parrett near Muchelney.

a bridge and cross the field to go through a gate to a lane. Turn left to walk through Muchelney Ham and follow the lane to Muchelney village.

❻ At the junction bear left past the Manor to the T-junction in front of the old school. Turn right to follow the lane back to the church.

The market cross, Muchelney.

BUTLEIGH

Length: 6 miles

Getting There: Butleigh is a large village grouped around a network of lanes about 6 miles south of Glastonbury. From Glastonbury, Sub Road leads directly to the village or take the A39 and approach the village from the B3151 via Street. Approaching from the south via the A303, turn for Langport along the A372, turn right along the B3151 signed Somerton then right again along the B3153. Turn left signed Street and after about 1 mile turn right for Butleigh.

Parking: Drive into the village and take the turning into the High Street where there is roadside parking.

Map: OS Landranger 182 Weston-super-Mare & Bridgwater (GR 519338).

Surrounded by meadows, woods and orchards, Butleigh is a charming village. Most of the houses are built of light-coloured stone - locally quarried blue lias - and many are thatched. Facing a small green is a delightful row of 17th century cottages. At the north end of the village stands Butleigh Court, an impressive mansion built in mock-Gothic style by the Very Rev George Neville (he took the surname Grenville). His grandson Robert invented a forerunner of the car, the

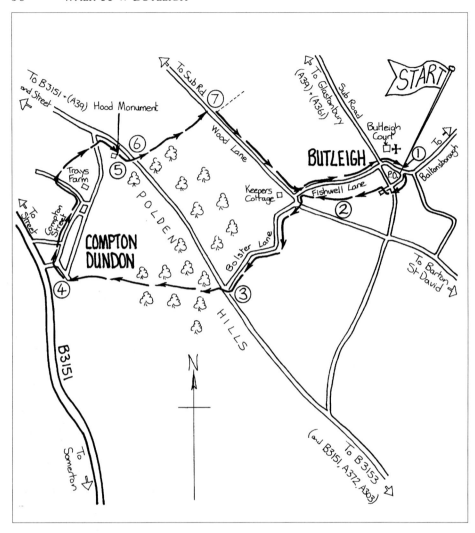

Grenville Steam Carriage. The mansion is now divided into apartments. But perhaps the village is better known as the home of the Rev Samuel Hood, rector from 1723, whose two sons, Samuel and Alexander, became famous admirals and received the titles of Viscount Hood and Viscount Bridport respectively.

The wonderful view from the Monument erected in memory of Viscount Hood is the highlight of this walk. The Monument stands high on the southern end of the Poldens, a ridge of hills running north-west across the Levels. From Butleigh, the route crosses the ridge and descends through a miniature gorge to Compton Dundon, another attractive stone-built village. There is a gentle climb

FOOD and DRINK

The Rose and Portcullis in Butleigh is well worth a visit for its good food and welcoming atmosphere.
Telephone: 01458 850287.

to the Monument before field paths and lanes lead back to Butleigh. Although part of the route follows lanes, these quiet grassy-edged ways around Butleigh, bordered with hedges bright with flowers, provide excellent walking.

THE WALK
❶ From the High Street, walk up Water Lane to leave the green on your left and the post office on your right. The lane bears right between thatched cottages to Sub Road. Cross over and continue ahead down the lane marked St James Square. Just past the no-through-road sign turn right to follow the footpath over two stiles. Bear left with a hedge and small stream on your left. Cross a stile and keep ahead over an orchard. Cross the next stile and continue keeping the hedge on your left. In the distance rise the wooded slopes of the Poldens.

❷ Across the next stile the path bears a little to the right over the field. Aim to cross to a point which appears to be to the

A peaceful scene in Compton Dundon.

right of a house and you will arrive at a stile leading into Fishwell Lane. Turn left to a T-junction with Wood Lane. Bear left for just a few yards then turn right up Bolster Lane, which winds left then right as it ascends the hillside. Look back for wide views over Butleigh in the valley of the Brue to Glastonbury Tor and the Mendip Hills.

❸ Cross over the main road and take the bridleway a little to the right which descends the wooded hillside to the right of a steep cleft threaded by a tiny stream. When the path divides keep along the right-hand path which rises a little then continues downhill, always keeping the stream on the left. Go through a gate to follow the path between high hedges wreathed in wild clematis.

❹ At the crosstrack turn right, pass a lane on the right. Turn right down the next lane, Compton Street. Keep ahead past the no-through-road sign and follow the lane as it bears left past Trays Farm. Continue

ahead for about 250 yards to a wide hedged grass path (unsigned) on the right. Turn right to follow this uphill and through the trees to meet a road. Cross over and take the footpath ahead signed for the Hood Monument. The path bears right through the woods to an open grassy area. Turn right to walk up to the Monument, a tall Tuscan column crowning the ridge. Looking back, the Monument is directly in line with Glastonbury Tor. Below the ridge, the Levels stretch westwards to the faint blue line of the Quantock Hills.

❺ With the Monument on your right continue along the path, which shortly meets a road. Cross the stone stile, cross the road and go over the stile on the other side signed Wood Lane.

❻ Ignore the track into the wood on the right but turn right round the edge of a field to the left of the wood. Bear left round the field, keeping the wood on your right, downhill to a stile by a gate. Cross and keep ahead, the wood still on your right. Just before a belt of woodland turn right over a stile then bear left, with the hedge on the left. Follow the hedge as it curves right then bear left to resume your former heading and cross a stile into Wood Lane.

❼ Turn right to follow Wood Lane for almost a mile. Pass the Keeper's Cottage and turn left down the next lane, Fishwell Lane. This time take the lane ahead into Butleigh and cross the road to follow the High Street back to your car.

SOUTH CADBURY

Length: 4½ miles

Getting there: South Cadbury is ½ mile south of the A303 between Wincanton and Ilchester. Turn off the A303 for South Cadbury and follow the sign for the car park through the village.

Parking: In the village car park. Pass the Red Lion pub and church on the right and a sign on the right indicates the turning into the car park on the left.

Map: OS Landranger 183 Yeovil & Frome (GR 632255).

Set in beautiful surroundings and built of golden stone, South Cadbury is a charming old-world village. The church dates from the 14th century and has an impressive tower with a stair turret, pinnacles and gargoyles. Inside, in the splay of one of the windows, is a wall painting of a bishop in cope and mitre, possibly St Thomas à Becket to whom the church is dedicated. Other interesting buildings include the Georgian old rectory and thatched Castle Farm House dated 1687. But South Cadbury has a special appeal. Lying in the shadow of one of Britain's mightiest hill forts, Cadbury Castle, the village is closely linked to the mysterious world of Arthur,

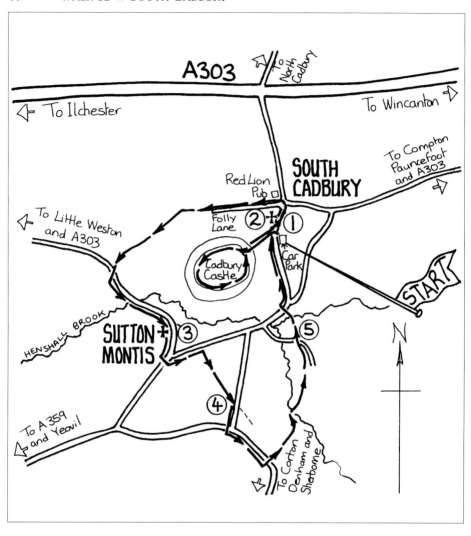

the great Celtic chieftain whose exploits in the Dark Ages have captured the imagination of all subsequent generations. It is possible that this admittedly shadowy figure made Cadbury Castle - named Camelot by later writers - his headquarters, and that he fought his last battle, Camlann, in the fields close by.

Did Arthur really exist? Elizabeth Jenkins in her book *The Mystery of King Arthur* argues convincingly that he did. But whatever view we take, enough factual evidence remains to prove that after the departure of the Roman legions in AD410 left Britain defenceless, some charismatic Celtic warrior later led a band of his countrymen against the invading hordes of

Saxons. Towards the end of the century, he defeated the Saxons in twelve battles culminating in a great victory at Mount Badon. Cadbury Castle, guarding the approaches to south-east Somerset, was ideally placed to be the headquarters of such a chieftain. Excavations between 1966-70, under the direction of Leslie Alcock, uncovered the remains of a great early 6th century feasting hall as well as defences on the hill fort. These are detailed in his book *By South Cadbury is That Camelot: Excavations at Cadbury Castle 1966 - 70.*

This is a walk in Arthur's footsteps. From the village we climb a track once known as Arthur's lane to the top of the hill fort to enjoy magnificent views over the Somerset Levels to the Quantock Hills. To the north-west rises the cone of Glastonbury Tor crowned by its tower. Looking south a swirl of downland encloses a secret valley. After descending the hill, the route takes lanes and field paths to visit another old-world village, Sutton Montis, and explore the countryside surrounding the fort.

THE WALK

❶ Turn right from the car park and take the track on the left just after the first house to climb the side of the hill fort. Go through a gate and continue through a dip in the wooded slopes of the lower ramparts. After about 20 yards a track on the left leads up

to a cattle trough and a few yards before the trough you will see a small bowl on the left surmounted by an arch, King Arthur's Well. When you reach the great oval plateau on the top of the fort it is rewarding to walk round the ramparts. In some places the four encircling banks with their dividing ditches reach a height of 40 feet. These immense fortifications were begun in the Iron Age and protected a flourishing and sophisticated community but they were strengthened around 500 AD, the time of Arthur.

Retrace your steps downhill to the village and turn left to pass the church on the left.

❷ Turn left down Folly Lane beside the Red Lion. The lane becomes a track and bears right. Cross the stile, bear left and continue over fields and stiles keeping the hedge on your left. When you reach a stile on the left, cross and bear right to continue with the hedge now on the right. The track kinks right to meet a lane. Turn left to follow the lane into Sutton Montis which you will see ahead cradled in the downs. The steep slopes of the hill fort tower above orchards as you approach the village. The church of the Holy Trinity has an exquisite Norman chancel arch. Walk through the village to a lane on the left signed for South Cadbury.

❸ Turn left and continue past a narrow track on the right to a footpath sign on the right signed Whitcombe. Turn right through a gate and over a stile. There is no clear path over the field ahead but keep straight on, aiming just to the left of a barn on the other side. Cross the stile and continue over the next field bearing a little left. Double stiles now lead to a lane.

❹ Turn right to follow the lane to a T-junction. Bear left, signed Corton Denham, and continue for about 200 yards. Just before the village sign turn left following the footpath sign for South Cadbury. Walk across the field to a track on the other side to the left of a belt of low woodland. Turn left along this track for about 80 yards to a stile on the right. Cross and walk through the trees and over a small wooden bridge. Over the field ahead a little to your left you will see a gate at the foot of the hillside. Cross to the gate and bear left with the

---

PLACES of INTEREST

Haynes Motor Museum at Sparkford houses over 200 vintage, veteran and classic cars and motorcycles. Open every day 9.30 am to 5.30 pm. Telephone: 01963 40804.

---

hillside on your right. Continue, keeping to the left of a wire fence and cross a stile on the right. Bear left over the corner of a lane.

❺ Keep straight ahead aiming to the left of a house. The path dips to cross a plank bridge then climbs to cross a stile and meet a lane. Turn right to follow the lane back to South Cadbury and the car park on the right.

Looking west from the ramparts of Cadbury Castle.

HINTON ST GEORGE

Length: 4½ miles

Getting there: Hinton St George is in South Somerset, a few miles north of Crewkerne. The best approach is from the north via the A303. Follow the sign from the	A303, drive through Lopen village and turn right for Hinton St George down Lopen Road. At the road junction in the village turn right into the High Street.	**Parking:** In the High Street. **Map:** OS Landranger 193 Taunton & Lyme Regis (GR 421128).

The Southern Uplands, running east from the slopes of the Blackdowns to form Somerset's border with Dorset, are a magical range of tumbled hills threaded by tiny streams. Here you find some of the county's most beautiful villages built of mellow golden stone quarried from nearby Ham Hill. One of the finest must be Hinton St George. The village lies along the crest of a ridge well away from the beaten track. It was owned until recently by the Poulett family who had held the manor of Hinton for over 500 years. The wide High Street is lined with charming houses, many dating from the 17th or early 18th century, set behind raised pavements bright with

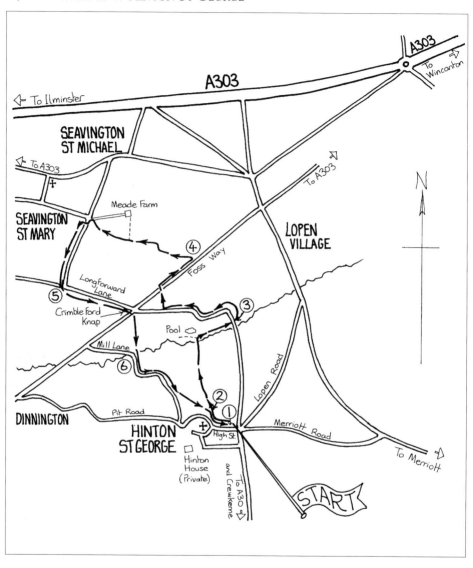

flowers. Old customs linger here, as you will discover if you visit the village on the last Thursday in October. This is Punkie Night. The children make Punkies, or candle-lanterns, out of hollowed-out mangolds and parade the streets singing. According to tradition this commemorates an attempt by the local ladies to retrieve their husbands unaccountably delayed at Chiselborough Fair!

This is a pleasant walk along quiet lanes and over meadows which are home for a variety of wildlife including roe deer and badgers. Growing in the hedgerows you

FOOD and DRINK

The Poulett Arms offers a warm welcome and good food and ales. Telephone: 01460 241716. There is also a friendly pub, The Docks, at Dinnington. Telephone: 01460 52397. If you wish to buy food for a picnic I recommend a visit to Hinton's excellent village shop.

will find several species of orchid, and spike-headed teasels which used to be cultivated for brushing up the knap in the cloth industry. The route follows part of the Roman Foss Way before returning to the village along a lane giving splendid views over the southern hills.

THE WALK

❶ Walk up the High Street leaving the pub, the Poulett Arms, on your right, towards the medieval stepped preaching cross at the road junction. The 16th century house to the left of the cross, known as the Priory, was probably once a manor. With the cross on your left, follow the road round to the right. After a few yards, opposite the lane to the church, turn right, down a narrow hedged footpath signed 'Underhill ⅔ mile'. The path bears left (ignore a gate on the right) and dips down steps to a small wooden gate.

❷ Go through the gate and take the

The view over the Somerset Levels from Hinton St George.

PLACES of INTEREST

Perry's Cider Mills at Dowlish Wake sell traditional Somerset cider made from apples grown in local orchards. It is open all the year every day except Sunday afternoons. Telephone: 01460 52681. The gardens of Elizabethan **Barrington Court** are open March to September daily except Friday 11 am to 5.30 pm. Telephone: 01460 241938. A visit to **Cricket St Thomas** wildlife park makes a splendid day out. Open April to October daily 10 am to 6 pm; November to March 10 am to 5 pm or dusk. Telephone: 01460 30755.

footpath indicated straight on down the field with a hedge close on the right. (The path to the left is your return route.) Cross the stile and continue ahead with the hedge on the left. Over the next stile keep ahead, the hedge now on the right. Over the next stile the path leads over a small bridge to a pond. Turn right to leave the pond on your left and walk beside the stream to cross a stile into Summer Lane.

❸ Bear left to follow this grass-bordered lane for about ½ mile to a sign on the right, 'Foss Way ⅙ mile'. Turn right over the stile and walk beside the field to cross another stile and meet the Foss Way - now a narrow road. Bear right along the Foss Way for about ⅓ mile and look for a stile on the left.

❹ Turn left over the stile and walk beside the field, a hedge on the right, to a stile on the right. Cross and bear left to continue the same heading, the hedge on the left. Cross a small bridge. On a rise on the right stands Meade Farm. From the bridge keep straight ahead to another stile. (This may be overgrown. If so, walk a few yards right and go through the gate on the left.) Continue with the hedge on the right and follow it round to the right to join a lane leading left to Seavington St Mary. Turn left for only a few yards over a small bridge then immediately left again to head south along another quiet lane. The lane sinks between high banks hung with trailing ivy and hart's tongue ferns. These sunken lanes are one of the delights of this part of Somerset. The lane climbs to emerge on top of a ridge giving a splendid view of the valley we have crossed, with the houses of Hinton St George crowning the hillside beyond. The tiny cluster of houses in a dip to the right is Dinnington village. On the horizon are the steep slopes of Windwhistle Hill. Follow the lane to a T-junction.

❺ Turn left to follow Longforward Lane and meet the Foss Way at Crimbleford Knap. Cross straight over and take the footpath ahead marked 'Hinton St George 1 mile'. Continue with the hedge on the right until you come to a gate just before the hedge bears left. Go through the gate and walk straight ahead down the field to go through two gates which open into Mill Lane.

❻ Keep ahead along Mill Lane over the valley. Just before the lane starts to climb the ridge turn left along a track signed Hinton St George. Continue to an iron gate on the right. Go through the gate and climb half-left diagonally up the hill to meet your earlier route by the small wooden gate. Retrace your steps along the footpath, turning left to pass the Cross and return to the High Street.

MONTACUTE

Length: 4½ miles

Getting there: Montacute is 4 miles west of Yeovil. The best approach is via the A303. Turn for Montacute along the A3088 and follow the signs to the village.	Parking: Drive into the village past the church on the right and park in the former market place, the Borough, which is round the next corner on the right.	Maps: OS Landrangers 183 Yeovil & Frome and 193 Taunton & Lyme Regis (GR 498169).

Montacute is one of Somerset's gems, a golden Ham stone village nestling in a grassy combe at the foot of one of Europe's most extensive hill forts. It takes its name from the Latin term for the conical hill west of the village, 'mons acutus'. The hill, now named after St Michael, was sacred to the Saxons because in 1035 a cross was found buried there. When Robert, the Norman Count of Mortain, built a castle on the top, they rebelled. Although they were defeated, the Saxons had their revenge as Robert was later obliged to found a Cluniac Priory in the village to make amends for a charge of treason and his castle was used as a quarry! Today the hill is crowned by an

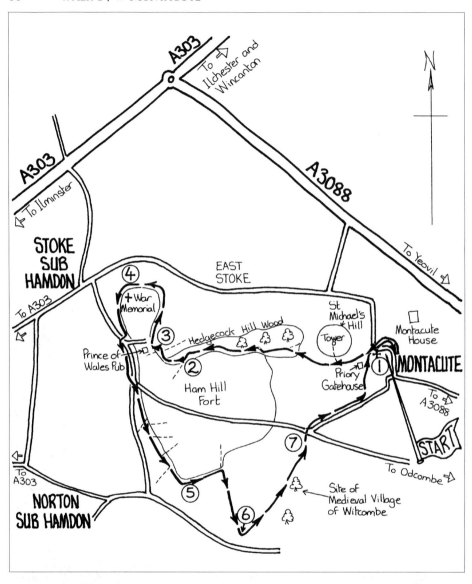

18th century tower. The magnificent Priory gatehouse and the monks' dovecot and fishpond can still be seen close to the village church which also dates from Norman times. East of the village is Montacute House, home of the Phelips family for 300 years, now owned by the National Trust.

Choose a clear day for this walk to enjoy the wonderful views along the route which takes woodland paths to the top of Ham Hill. The best view of all is from the War

THE WALK

❶ From the Borough turn left into Middle Street, leaving the entrance to Montacute House on your right. Turn left again just past the church then right, following the footpath sign for Hedgecock Hill Wood. The Priory gatehouse is on the left. Go through a gate to climb the track ahead and at the fork continue along the left-hand path which curves round the hillside. Pass a stile on the left and cross the stile ahead to climb a woodland path, sunk deep between banks hung with hart's tongue ferns. Turn left at the crosspath and continue up the main path to a stile on the right. Cross this then bear left to resume your former

Memorial which crowns the north-west corner of Ham Hill - all central Somerset from the Quantocks east to the Mendips is spread at your feet. We return to Montacute through one of the loveliest places in the county, a hidden valley, the site of a vanished medieval village.

A War Memorial crowns the north-west corner of Ham Hill.

heading. The path weaves through the trees with the upper rampart of the hill fort on your left.

❷ The path dips steeply and divides. Navigate carefully here! Do not take the left-hand path which climbs quickly to the open space at the top of the fort. Take the right-hand path which drops steeply downhill. Ignore all circular walk signs and take the first path on the left. The path curves right into a valley to a crossways. Take the path straight ahead which leads uphill to stone steps on the left. Climb these to emerge opposite the front of the Prince of Wales pub.

❸ Bear right and follow the narrow path along the top of the hill fort ramparts. Keep to the highest point as the ramparts curve left to enjoy the splendid views.

❹ A few yards before the War Memorial you will see an iron seat a few yards downhill on the right. Walk down to the seat and turn left along a grassy path tracing the hillside. At the road turn right, then left at the T-junction. Continue past a lane on

the right and after about 20 yards follow the sign on the right to continue along the top of the embankment. Bear a little left over a car park to continue along the wide path just to the right of a litter bin. Continue to a fork and take the right-hand path, a fence on the left. At the next fork keep straight ahead along the left-hand path. Continue along the edge of the hill fort. Continue past a gate on the left and keep straight on as another path bears left. At the next fork continue along the left-hand path, keeping your height.

❺ The path drops steeply to a crosstrack. Turn right through the edge of woods with a valley on your left. Just before you reach a track at the foot of the hill look for a gate on the left signed Witcombe Lane.

❻ Turn left through the gate and bear left up the valley leaving a gate and wood on the right. Keep to the main path, aiming for the skyline to the right of some farm buildings. Some trees on the right and grass-covered mounds mark the site of Witcombe medieval village. The path curves right up the hill then left through gates to a road.

❼ Cross straight over Hollow Lane and take the footpath to the left of the lane. Cross stiles and continue downhill with the lane on your right. Below you have a superb view of Montacute village. Cross a stile on the right and turn left along the track signed Montacute church. Turn right past the church to return to the Borough.

BURRINGTON

Length: 4 miles

Getting there: Burrington lies in the shelter of the northern slopes of the Mendips just south of the A368 from Bath to Weston-super-Mare. Approaching from the west, turn for Burrington about 2 miles east of the Churchill junction. Approaching	from Bristol take the A38 south to the Churchill junction. **Parking:** Drive into the village and park in the square. The church and school are on your right.	**Map:** OS Landranger 182 Weston-super-Mare & Bridgwater (GR 479594).

The great limestone plateau of the Mendips runs across northern Somerset for 20 miles from the countryside near Frome to the Severn Estuary at Weston-super-Mare. The hills rise to their highest point, over 1,000 feet, at Black Down. From the summit, wooded slopes fall gently towards the Avon valley. The small village of Burrington nestles at their foot. Only a ¼ mile away from a busy road you suddenly come across this charming cluster of stone-built houses with gardens bright with flowers, spilling into the road and tumbling over low stone walls. The church is one of

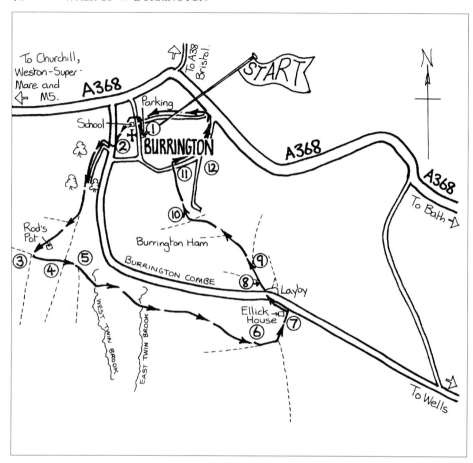

my favourites. The exterior is decorated with parapets and battlements and a graceful spire crowns the tower adjoining the north aisle. Inside, the beautifully timbered roofs are supported by carved angels.

South of the village a deep gorge, Burrington Combe, cuts through the limestone. In the 18th century the Rev Augustus Toplady sheltered from a storm in a cleft in a rock in the combe, which inspired him to compose his famous hymn *Rock of Ages*. You can drive through the

combe along the B3134 but I have planned this walk to follow upland paths along the top to enjoy the wonderful views, north to Bristol tucked comfortably in the Avon gorge and west over the Severn Estuary to the hills of Wales. A quiet path beside a low stone wall hung with ferns leads through the meadows back to the village.

THE WALK

❶ Leave the church and the front of the school on your left and turn left down the narrow path that runs past the side of the

FOOD and DRINK

The Burrington Inn, beside the B3134 in Burrington Combe, serves light snacks and drinks throughout the day in the bar and full meals in the restaurant. Telephone: 01761 462227.

school. Go through a small iron gate into the school playing field. Bear half-left diagonally over the grass to go through a wooden gate on the other side. Continue diagonally over the next field to go through a gate to the road, the B3134.

❷ Turn left beside the road for about 200 yards then turn right up a narrow metalled lane between high hedges. Keep to the lane as it bears left and climbs past a footpath sign on the left. Pass another footpath sign on the right and follow the lane as it rises through beech and oak woods. The lane passes between concrete gate posts and becomes more stony. Continue past a track on the left opposite a wooden gate on the right and shortly after keep to the lane past a track on the right marked 'Private'. The lane becomes a stony track as it leaves the woods to emerge on the open slopes of Black Down, which rise smooth and green on your left. Black Down is an isolated outcrop of old red sandstone so the track at

The path over Burrington Ham looking towards the Avon valley.

this lower level makes its way through heathland thick with bracken and dotted with gorse and rowan. The large dip on your left is the entrance to Rod's Pot, one of the many caves which honeycomb the Mendips. Keep on to a post marked with bridleway signs in front of a crossing track.

❸ Turn left over the moor with the slopes of Black Down now rising on your right. Over on your left are the undulating bands of gleaming white limestone forming the opposite side of Burrington Combe, and beyond them glimpses of the Severn Estuary and the Welsh hills.

❹ Continue straight over the crosspath, following an unmarked path. (It is a right-of-way.)

❺ Shortly after, the path divides. Take the left-hand path which drops steeply to cross West Twin Brook. Ignore all paths to right and left, cross the brook and keep to the path as it bears left then resumes its former heading over the moor. The path dips again to cross East Twin Brook. As before, keep to the main path ignoring all paths to left and right. Continue for about ¾ mile to a post marked with bridleway signs in front of a crosstrack.

❻ Bear left for about 100 yards to another crosstrack and post. Turn left to follow the wider track downhill. Pass Ellick House to meet the B3134.

❼ Turn left beside the road for about 100 yards to a layby on the right, just before the

PLACES of INTEREST

From the car park in Burrington Combe you can walk to the **Rock of Ages**. The **Cheddar Gorge** is in easy reach by car. For information telephone: 01934 742343.

road makes a sharp left bend. Cross the layby, ignore the grassy path on the right and follow the white stony track leading uphill just to the right of the road. This climbs away from the road up Burrington Ham.

❽ Ignore the narrow footpath on the left and keep on following the bridleway sign for a few more yards.

❾ The path, now grassy, divides. Take the left-hand path. You are now walking in limestone country and in summer the short turf is starred with yellow rock roses and scented with thyme and marjoram. The path descends through woods and when it divides take the right-hand path. Ignore all paths and tracks to right and left until you see a post on the right marked with a blue arrow bridleway sign.

❿ Bear right at the post to descend to meet a lane.

⓫ Turn right along the lane for about 300 yards to meet another lane.

⓬ Turn left down this lane to the A368. Bear left round the front of a house then turn left up Burrington Lane to return to the village.

PRIDDY

Length: 6 miles

Getting there: Priddy is a small village high on the Mendip plateau about 6 miles west of Cheddar. The best approach is via the B3135. Turn for the village off the B3135	and continue for about a mile past the church to the village green. **Parking:** By the green or in front of the New Inn.	**Map:** OS Landranger 182 Weston-super-Mare & Bridgwater (GR 527511).

Priddy is the most romantic village I know and also the spookiest! This isolated cluster of grey stone houses nestling in a hollow of the Mendips has a character all its own. Sheep fairs are held in August on the green where a thatched hurdle stack stands as a reminder throughout the year. All around the village there are Bronze Age burial mounds and Neolithic circles. Iron Age people may have been the first to mine lead here, an industry which flourished at various times until the last mine closed in 1908 leaving disturbed earth known as 'gruffy ground'. And there is a tradition that Christ walked these hills as a boy accompanying his uncle on trading

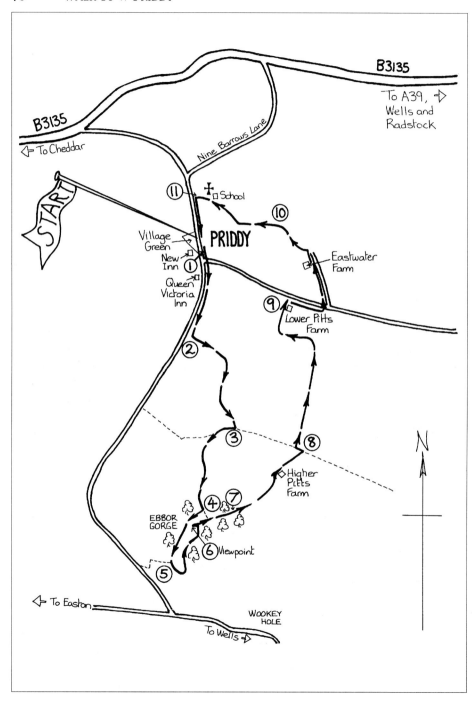

FOOD and DRINK

The New Inn facing the green provides excellent home-made food and well kept beers. Telephone: 01749 676465.

expeditions, a legend recalled by William Blake in his famous hymn *Jerusalem*.

South of Priddy the Mendip hills rise in a steep scarp above The Levels intersected by ravines carved by rivers over 270 million years ago. The most beautiful is the Ebbor Gorge. Here there are no roads only a footpath which winds up the heavily wooded valley between towering cliffs. The walk crosses fields then takes this path before climbing steps to the top of the Mendip plateau to enjoy splendid views and returning to Priddy. *(The path near the top of the gorge is rough and slippery so take care and wear strong shoes or boots.)*

THE WALK

❶ Leave the front of the New Inn on your right and turn right down the lane marked 'Single track road with passing places'. Pass the Queen Victoria Inn.

❷ After ½ mile turn left over an iron stile by a wooden post indicating the West Mendip Way to Wookey Hole. Keep straight ahead with a wall on your left and at the top of the field follow the wall round to the right. Cross a stile on the right and continue ahead for about 100 yards, then turn left over a stone stile to resume your former heading with the wall now on your right and a fence on your left. Follow the fence as it bears left then cross a stile to meet a crossing track.

❸ Turn right down the hedged bridleway signed Wookey Hole. After about 200 yards cross a stile on the left and keep ahead with a wall, then a fence, on the left, to the corner of the field. Bear right, the fence still on your left, for about 50 yards to a stile on the left. Cross the stile. There is no visible path at this point but keep straight on over the field towards the skyline and you will see a stile ahead in the stone wall. Cross the stile and walk down the meadow, bearing a little right to cross a stile on your right. Turn left, signed for the Ebbor Gorge.

❹ Descend the narrow path which drops steeply to meet a path at the head of the gorge. Turn right to follow the path through dramatic scenery. It is easy going at first but soon the path narrows, becoming steep and rocky as it picks its way between the cliffs, passing caves which provided shelter for Neolithic man. Continue for about ½ mile keeping to the same path which becomes easier as the gorge widens.

❺ Pass a path on the right signed for the car park and after a few yards turn left by a wooden post signed Priddy. Climb the wooden steps up the side of the gorge. The path bears right and becomes less steep before turning left and climbing more steps to meet a crosstrack.

❻ The walk turns right here but first turn left past the notice ' Caution – cliff edge 50 yards' to enjoy a magnificent view west over The Levels. Retrace your steps past the notice and continue straight on and over a crosstrack to leave the woods over a stile.

❼ Follow the path up the meadow to go

Looking down at the Ebbor Gorge.

through a gate. Continue keeping a fence on the left. The path bears half-left beside the fence. Cross some wooden bars beside a gate and continue to go through a gate and down a track over a stile in the direction of Higher Pitts Farm. Turn left then right, round the farm, as the signs direct, to join a track. Follow the track through a gate and keep on for about 30 yards to a crossing track.

❽ Bear left for just a few yards then turn right over a cattle grid down a lane signed 'Private road, footpath only'. Follow this for about a mile until after bends to left and right it passes Lower Pitts Farm to the Wells road.

❾ Turn right beside the road for about ¼ mile then turn left up the first lane on the left. Pass Eastwater Farm on the left then turn immediately left along the footpath signed for Priddy church. Walk over the caravan site to cross a stile into a meadow. Keep ahead for a few yards then bear right to cross a ladder stile. Continue bearing a little left through a gap in a wall.

❿ Turn left to walk beside a field and cross into the next field. On the hillside a little to your right you will see Priddy church. Bear half right down the field towards the church. Cross two stiles and walk up the bank to go over a stone stile by Priddy school. Follow the path to the road and turn left to return to the village green.

NUNNEY

Length: 4½ miles

Getting there: Nunney is 4 miles south-west of Frome. Turn for Nunney off the A361.

Parking: Parking in the market place is limited to two hours. There is roadside parking in the village but at busy times turn left just past the market place then turn right past the shop, where there is ample parking beside the road to the castle.

Map: OS Landranger 183 Yeovil & Frome (GR 737458).

Nunney is tucked in a wooded valley at the southern foot of the Mendip Hills. Built of grey-green local stone, the attractive houses and cottages, many dating from the 17th century, cluster around the ruins of a moated medieval castle. This massive rectangular tower was built by Sir John de la Mare in 1373. Held for the King in the Civil War, it was destroyed by victorious Parliamentary troops. Opposite the castle stands All Saints church, famous for its fine medieval effigies and 15th century screen. The Nunney Brook runs through the village beside green lawns. Until the mid-

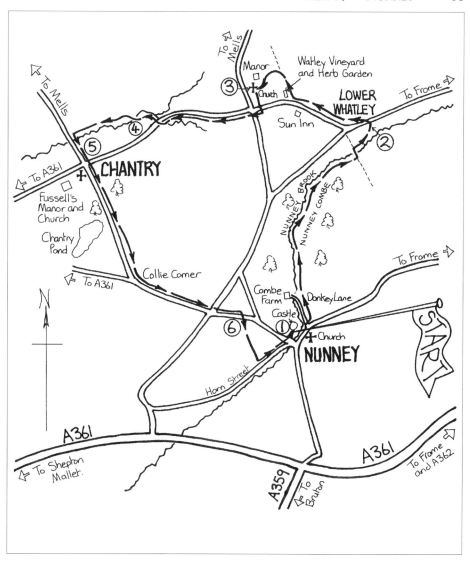

19th century it provided power for the local cloth industry and some former weavers' cottages still have square holes in the ceilings through which the lengths of cloth hung as they were woven.

This relaxing walk follows the wooded valley of the Nunney Brook to Whatley where you will find a vineyard and herb garden in the grounds of an old rectory. We visit Chantry, an interesting village built by James Fussell around his manor and edge-tool works in 1825, before taking quiet lanes back to Nunney.

THE WALK

❶ Walk up the main street, Frome Road, leaving the George Inn on your right. Pass the cross and take the next turning on the left, known locally as Donkey Lane. Keep ahead past a turning on the right, through a gateway leading to the asphalt drive to Combe Farm. Follow the drive to the point where it bears left to the farm. Now keep straight ahead over a stile to follow a tree-shaded footpath along Nunney Combe with the Nunney Brook on your left. After about ¼ mile the path meets a crosstrack. Turn left to cross an iron-railed bridge, then turn right over a stile and continue along the combe with the brook now on

your right. The path climbs beside a small stone bridge. Cross the stile and keep ahead up the track past the houses to a road by Park Farm at Lower Whatley.

❷ Turn left to follow the road through the village. The road rises past a turning to Nunney then descends to leave the Sun Inn on the left. A little further on, as the road

Nunney Castle.

curves left, you will see the entrance to Whatley vineyard and herb garden on your right. Bear right to leave the entrance on your left and follow the asphalt lane with a stone wall on your left. Pass a cottage on the right and keep straight ahead to an asphalt drive. Turn right to walk between houses and continue along a narrow path to cross a stile into a field. Bear left with a fence on your left to cross a stile. Bear half-left to cross another stile towards Whatley church. Just before the gate to the farm beside the church go through a gate on the left, then over a stone stile on the right to enter the churchyard. The farm, once a manor, retains its medieval gatehouse. The church of St George dates from the 13th century.

❸ From the south porch of the church walk down to the road, turn right, cross the main road and follow the lane ahead signed for Chantry. Continue for about ½ mile to cross a bridge in a valley. Immediately after the bridge you will see two footpath signs beyond a gate on the right. Turn right through two gates following the sign that points straight ahead. The path curves left over the grass round a low bank to run to the left of a stream in a wooded valley. Continue for about 50 yards.

❹ Look carefully for a stile a few yards from the path on the right leading into the wood. Turn right over the stile and follow the streamside path with the stream on your left. You may have to pick your way carefully in some places but the path is generally easy to follow. Cross a stile and

> ### PLACES of INTEREST
>
> Whatley's 4 acre **vineyard** and cruciform **herb garden** are open from 1st April to 30th September, Wednesday to Sunday, 10am to 1pm and 2pm to 6pm. Telephone: 01373 836467.

continue with a quarry fence on your right, over another stile to a lane by Chantry Farm. Turn left to walk to the crossroads in Chantry. Our way is straight over down the lane for Nunney but to see James Fussell's great house and his church (designed by Gilbert Scott and complete with angels grasping edge-tools) make a detour right and go through the door in the wall on the left. From the church there is a splendid view over Nunney Combe to Cley Hill and the Wiltshire downs.

❺ Return to the crossroads and follow the attractive lane leading downhill past the lake and waterfall which once provided power for the Fussell mills. Keep to the lane until it climbs to meet a road. Turn left at Collie Corner, continue to cross over the main road and follow the lane ahead for about 200 yards.

❻ Turn right over the stile by a footpath sign and walk straight ahead with a fence on the left. The field path descends to a stile. Cross the stile to a road in Nunney. Turn left to walk down the road – Primrose Hill – and along Horn Street past the Mill, rows of weavers' cottages and the old lock-up. Turn right for the market place, or left then right past the shop to the castle to return to your car.

BECKINGTON

Length: 4½ miles

Getting there: Beckington is a large village in north-east Somerset about 3 miles north of Frome. It is now bypassed by both the main roads which used to meet in the village, the A36 Bath–Warminster and the A361 Frome–Trowbridge. Approaching from the east, leave the A36 following the sign for Beckington. Drive into the village and turn left into the main street just past the Woolpack Inn. Approaching from the north follow the sign for Beckington and keep straight on down the main street of the village. Follow the same directions to leave the A361 which joins the A36 at the bypass.

Parking: There is ample roadside parking in the main street of the village.

Map: OS Landranger 183 Yeovil & Frome (GR 801519).

Take time to enjoy a stroll round this attractive village. Fine houses with mellow stone gables and mullioned and transomed windows give way to rows of cottages, every one different from its neighbour. In the 13th century the establishment of fulling mills made the export of finished cloth possible and the villagers of Beckington prospered, processing and weaving wool brought from the Mendip Hills and the

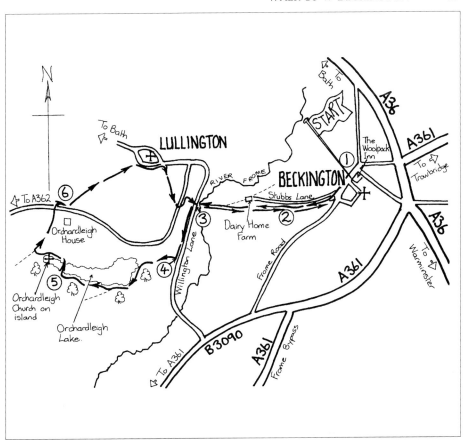

Wiltshire downs. This prosperity is reflected in the church with its magnificent Norman tower and fine open timber roof. Another interesting building is Beckington Castle – not a castle at all but a many-gabled house with mullioned windows and an impressive porch.

This walk through pleasantly undulating countryside will be enjoyed by all the family. Field paths cross the Frome valley to the shores of the beautiful lake at Orchardleigh. The return route includes a visit to the tiny hamlet of Lullington, famous for its 12th century church.

THE WALK

❶ Leaving the front of the Woolpack Inn on your left walk up the main street. Pass Beckington House on the right and turn immediately right down Stubbs Lane which leads into open countryside. Pass the sign for Dairy Home Farm and continue to a cattle grid with a small gate and footpath sign on the left.

❷ Do not continue down the drive to the farm but go through the gate and keep straight ahead over the grass to a stile marked with a yellow arrow footpath sign.

Cross and follow the path leading diagonally downhill to the next stile. Continue over the next field, with a fence on the left, and over another stile. Keep ahead over another field and stile to emerge on a narrow strip of meadow. Walk over the meadow and cross the iron bridge spanning the Frome river. You will see a stile on the right which takes you over a stone wall into Lullington Lane. Cross the lane to a post indicating several footpaths.

❸ Turn left to follow the sign that indicates a path running over rough grass parallel with the lane. Cross the stile and keep straight ahead (ignore the direction of

the arrow indicating another path). Orchardleigh golf course is on your right. Continue with the hedge and lane on the left to a crosspath.

❹ Turn right uphill along the side of the golf course to follow the edge of a wood for about 50 yards. The path then bears left into the wood, crosses a stream and climbs

Looking across the lake to Orchardleigh House.

to continue through the trees with the stream on the right. A rise brings you to the left of a brick-built bridge. Now you have a beautiful view of Orchardleigh lake, a haven for wildlife. To the right of the bridge is a small 18th century temple. Turn left to walk beside the lake. On the hillside to your right stands Orchardleigh House, an impressive mansion built in Gothic style in the mid-19th century by William Duckworth, a wealthy lawyer. Follow the path as it bears right along the lakeside. When the path divides still keep to the lakeside (the right-hand path). After about ½ mile the path turns right to face the lake.

❺ Follow the path right, then bear left to cross two bridges over the lake to the meadow on the other side. Turn left with the lake now on your left and keep ahead to a small iron gate on the left. Cross a small bridge to go through another gate, then turn left to go over the bridge to the tiny church of St Mary the Virgin, on a wooded island at the head of the lake. We found the church locked but it is well worth a visit if only for its lovely setting. The poet, Henry Newbolt, is buried in the churchyard.

Retrace your steps over the bridge, turning right through the two small gates to the meadow. Turn left here and walk to meet a good track. Bear right up the track over the golf course (take care!) to a tarmac drive. Turn right along the drive past one post with yellow footpath signs to another signed post just beyond the approach to the gateway to Orchardleigh House.

❻ Turn left and bear diagonally right over the grass between the trees to a fence on the other side of the golf course. Look for a stile

crossing the fence a little to your right. Over the stile a clear path leads over the meadows to meet a lane. Turn right to follow the lane into Lullington village. Pass the village pump on the left and bear right round the cottages. Now turn immediately right down the lane marked with a no-through-road sign. After about 100 yards turn right, following the footpath sign, and follow the path through gates to meet the drive leading left to an entrance gate to the park. Turn left to walk down to a metal gate. Do not continue to the entrance which is private but before the gate, turn right to walk over the grass to rejoin your earlier route at the approach to Lullington Lane. Cross the lane to retrace the route over the stile and across the fields. As you approach Dairy House Farm keep to your former route which is the right-hand of the two paths indicated.

CHEW MAGNA

Length: 6½ miles

Getting there: Chew Magna is a large village beside the B3130, 6 miles south of Bristol. Approaching from the west turn for the village off the A38, approaching from the east turn off the A37.	**Parking:** In the village car park which is signed off the B3130. Drive down the side of the Pelican Inn (leaving the inn on your left) to the car park.	**Map:** OS Landranger 182 Weston-super-Mare & Bridgwater (GR 575631).

In medieval days Chew Magna was one of the administrative centres of the powerful Bishop of Bath and Wells and the people grew rich on the wool trade. There are signs of this prosperity still in the Georgian houses built of local red-brown stone, the high raised pavements and the church with its magnificent 15th century tower. Close to the church is a rare survival, the medieval Church House. Here the churchwardens used to provide food and drink for lively social gatherings to defray parish expenses.

Allow a full day to enjoy this walk beside the river Chew. Valley paths take you to Stanton Drew, famous for its circles

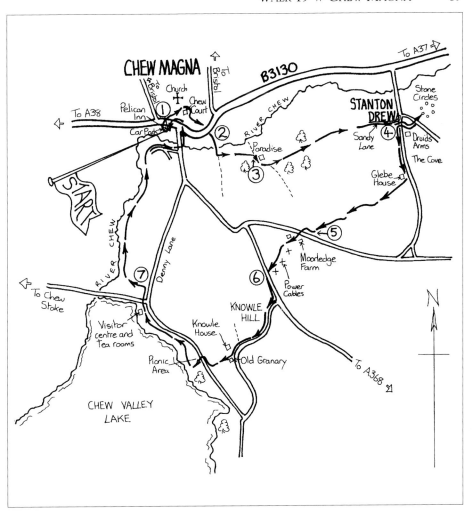

of standing stones dating from Neolithic times. An exciting discovery was made in 1997. Beneath the stones, archaeologists found nine concentric circles of wooden postholes, proving the existence of a huge temple twice the size of Stonehenge and probably 500 years older! From here your route leads to Chew Valley Lake, a beautiful expanse of water fringed with trees and rich in wildlife, with wide views over the Mendips along the way. The walk includes a ramble along the lake shore before returning to the village along the riverside.

THE WALK

❶ Return to the entrance to the car park, turn right and cross the road. Pass the Church House on your right and enter the churchyard. Turn right along the path to

FOOD and DRINK

The Pelican Inn serves excellent food and real ales. Telephone: 01275 332448. Chew Valley Lake Tea Shop is open every day from 16th March to 1st November, 10.30 am to 5.30 pm. The rest of the year it is open Wednesday to Sunday, 10.30 am to 4.30 pm. Telephone: 01275 333345.

leave the south porch of the church on your left. When the main path bears left keep straight on over a stile topped with an iron bar. The side of Chew Court and its garden wall are on your right. Follow the wall round to go past a gate and meet the drive to Chew Court. Turn left and walk down the drive to the road.

❷ Cross the road and climb the stile into a field. Keep ahead, with a hedge on the left, to cross a stile on the left before the Chew. Turn right over the river and another stile leads to a grassy path. With the river on your left follow the path to a division. Bear left, still keeping the river close on your left, to a gate marked with a 'two rivers' sign. Bear right before the gate, a hedge on your left, to a break in the hedge and low fence marked with a footpath sign. Cross the fence and follow the path down the field towards a cottage in a wooded dip aptly named Paradise. Go over a stile and a small bridge along a path through the trees to meet a track.

❸ Turn right and follow the track which bears left and becomes Sandy Lane as it passes houses in Stanton Drew. At the T-junction turn left for a few yards, then right to meet a lane. Bear right to the sign for Stanton Drew Stone Circle. Turn left as

the sign directs to a gate on the right which gives access to the meadows dotted with these huge stones. (See Places of Interest.)

❹ Retrace your steps to pass Sandy Lane on your right and continue up the road. Just past Glebe House on the right, turn right over a stile by a footpath sign. Keep ahead with a hedge on the right over fields and stiles until the path ceases by a gate on the right. Go through the gate and continue with the hedge on your left. The path rises to give wide views over the undulating countryside to the Mendip Hills. After about 200 yards look for a stile on the left. Cross this and continue with the hedge now on your right. Keep straight ahead downhill towards a house in the valley. Cross a stile and bear slightly left down the meadow towards a corner post with a yellow arrow footpath sign. From the post walk straight ahead down the field to go through a gate to a lane.

❺ Turn right down the lane to cross a stream. Turn left at the footpath sign following the track to Moorledge Farm. Pass the farm and cross a stile on the right to follow a narrow path which climbs to a double stile. Over the stile the meadow rises. On the left you will see a line of power cables. Walk up the field bearing a little left, aiming for the skyline just to the right of the cables. In the corner at the top of the field an iron gate opens into a lane.

PLACES of INTEREST

The **Stanton Drew Stone Circles** can be visited between 9 am and sunset. £1 entrance fee.

❻ Turn left along the lane for about 100 yards then turn right along a lane signed for Knowle Hill. The lane winds round Knowle Hill. Just past Knowle House turn right to cross the cattle grid and courtyard, past the Old Granary, to go through a gate on the left. Turn right to walk down the fields and over a stile towards Chew Valley Lake with a hedge on your right. A gate opens to a road. Turn right to walk the few yards to the sign for the picnic site. Follow the sign to the lake shore. The lake was created as a reservoir by Bristol Water in 1956. Turn right and follow the path over the car park and along the lake shore to another picnic site with a Visitor Centre and Tea Shop.

With the cafe on your left walk up to the road. Opposite, you will see Denny Lane with a footpath sign and stile on the corner. Cross the stile and walk up the field parallel with the lane to a metalled path.

❼ Turn left as the sign indicates. Before the Chew, turn right along a narrow path and follow the valley with the river on your left. As you approach Chew Magna, go through a gate to a T-junction. Turn right and at the division take the left-hand lane which leads to a road. Turn left to cross Tun Bridge and walk up to the village street. Turn left, then left again past the Pelican Inn back to your car.

Neolithic stone circles at Stanton Drew.

WELLOW

Length: 5 miles

<table>
<tr><td>Getting there: Wellow is 4 miles south of Bath. Approaching from the north or south turn off the A36 following the sign for Hinton Charterhouse and Wellow. Drive straight over the crossroads in Hinton Charterhouse and continue</td><td>along Wellow Lane for about 2 miles. Pass the church on the right and the Fox and Badger pub on the left, continue through the village and turn left following the Free Car Park sign.</td><td>Parking: In the village car park as above.

Map: OS Landranger 172 Bristol, Bath & surrounding area (GR 736581).</td></tr>
</table>

Wellow is an attractive village built of warm honey-coloured stone, beautifully situated on a south-facing hillside overlooking the Wellow Brook. The church is exceptionally light and uncluttered with magnificent carved timber roofs, an exquisite 15th century rood screen with a loft and gallery designed and erected in 1952, and 15th century frescoes. Among many interesting houses are the Manor, the mid-19th century school and the old granary.

The walk climbs from the village to follow a ridge with splendid views. A quiet

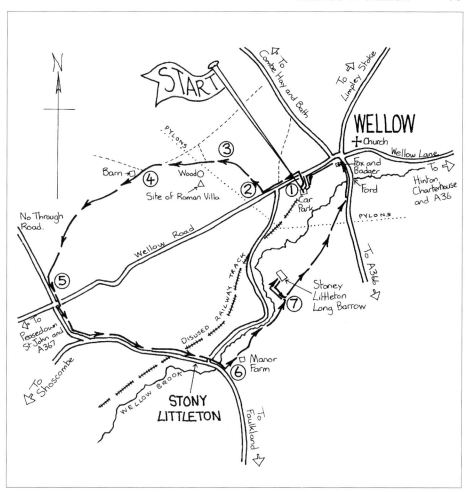

lane descends into the Wellow valley before a hillside bridleway leads back to the village, visiting on the way a 4,000 year old Neolithic burial chamber.

THE WALK

❶ Cross the car park to the entrance lane. Today, Wellow car park, high on a hillside overlooking the valley of the Wellow Brook, must be one of the most attractive in the West Country and it is hard to believe that steam trains of the Cam Valley branch line, linking Bath with Radstock, once ran straight across it! As you join the lane you pass one of the station buildings – now a house – still with its Victorian palings. Walk up to the main road through the village, turn left and continue past the last houses in the village. Ignore the first bridleway sign on the right.

❷ Turn right at the second bridleway sign

and continue through a gate. Climb the path ahead beside a field, with a hedge on the right. On the hillside on the left you will see a small wood. Below the wood, a brown scar on the open hillside marks the site of a Roman villa, one of several that flourished in these attractive river valleys close to Bath and the Foss Way.

❸ Follow the path as it curves left and go through a small gate on the right. Turn left and cross to a stile by a gate. The right-of-way leads over the stile then diagonally half-right up the field ahead, under the pylons, to a gate in the top left-hand corner where it meets a crosstrack. As there is no

> **FOOD and DRINK**
>
> The Fox and Badger offers good family meals in a welcoming atmosphere. Open all day on Friday and Saturday, Monday to Thursday 11.30 am to 2.30 pm and 6 pm to 11 pm, Sunday 12 noon to 10.30 pm. Telephone: 01225 832293.

clear path you may prefer not to cross the stile, but turn right and take the well-worn path uphill, a hedge on the left, to meet the crosstrack by a more direct route. Whichever route you follow, turn left to follow the crosstrack. The track runs along a ridge with wide views on either side, east to Cley Hill and the White Horse at

The entrance to Stoney Littleton Long Barrow, a neolithic burial chamber near Wellow.

Westbury and south and west over the Mendips. After about ¼ mile the path dips slightly and a track joins on the left in front of a large barn.

❹ Do not take the more obvious track downhill but turn left uphill to leave the barn on your right. Continue for about ½ mile to go over a crosstrack and through a gate. Walk up the field ahead, with a hedge on the right, to go through another gate and keep ahead, still with a hedge on the right. The next gate opens into a narrow lane.

❺ Turn left to follow the lane to meet the Wellow Road. Cross over and continue down the lane signed Shoscombe. When the lane bears right for Shoscombe, keep straight on down a lane signed Stony Littleton. The lane drops into the valley to pass the scattered houses of the village and cross the bridge over the disused railway. Ignore all byway and bridleway signs and continue over the Wellow Brook. Walk uphill for about 50 yards.

❻ Turn left, following the bridleway sign along a terraced hillside path with the brook running along the valley on your left. Pass Manor Farm on the right and keep ahead through a gate with a fence and hedge on the left. When the hedge bends left towards the river bear a little left to walk along the right-hand bank of the brook. Continue along the bank, past a footbridge and go over a stile. Climb the hillside ahead but before reaching the top look for a stile and sign for Stoney Littleton Long Barrow on the left.

❼ Turn left over the stile and keep ahead, with a hedge on the right, to a stile and another sign for the long barrow on the right. Cross and take the path ahead to see the barrow. Retrace your steps to the hillside path and continue uphill. Go through a small gate on your left and keep on uphill, a hedge on the right. A gate leads to a narrow hedged path and as you follow this downhill there is a fine view of Wellow on the hillside ahead. When the path meets a lane keep on downhill and bear left to cross the packhorse bridge over the Wellow Brook at the foot of Mill Street. Climb Mill Street and turn left to walk past the old manor and the pub back to your car.

ACKNOWLEDGEMENTS

As always I am grateful to the staff of Southampton and Totton libraries. I would also like to thank Tim Chambre of Portswood library and Sue Billinge and the staff of Taunton library. I received valuable information and assistance from Mrs Lynette Jenkins and the staff of the Tourist Information Bridgwater, Ros Taylor and the staff of Podimore Information Centre, and the staff of Minehead Information Centre. My thanks also to all at the Dunster Information Centre especially Beryl Priddle who helped to inspire me with her own love of Somerset. For historical information I am grateful to Elaine Amos, English Heritage, Historic Properties South West. John and Wendy Millett from Dinnington and Peter and Sue Knight provided me with information about Hinton St George and I am grateful to John Wratten and Jane Henderson for help with my chapter about Muchelney. For the kind hospitality I received at Muchelney I would like to thank Jeremy Filmer-Bennett. Crowcombe will always be a favourite village because I was made so welcome by Tony and Jan Allen (who also gave me information) and Graham and Jan Lamacraft. I would also like to thank all the patient people who tested these walks for me.

The photographs would not have been the same without the assistance of our friends Captain Dickie Snell and his wife Liz who provided much needed refreshments. As always I thank my friend, Mary Chambers, for her unfailing interest and support.

I would also like to thank Paula Leigh and all my friends at Countryside Books for helping to make writing this book such a pleasure. And finally my thanks to my husband Mike for checking the routes, taking the photographs and being my companion on every step of the way.